Praise for the Weird & Wacky Holiday Marketing Guide through the years ...

"This book is a fun way to market just about anything. Organized by month, with month-long holidays, week-long holidays, and then daily holidays. Most of the holidays are so obscure that most people wouldn't be aware they even exist. But that is the point: taking a weird and wacky holiday and making a fun marketing post with it.

"Behind the monthly holidays is a section with sample posters and additional ideas that can be transferred to any other holiday, a sample press release, as well as links to companies and social media sites that might also help.

"I have gone through and highlighted holidays I want to promote for fun next time they roll around. The title is all about having a little fun while you market and this book will not disappoint."
Pat Stanford, Author & Poet (2019 Edition)

"This is such a wonderful resource. I love how Ginger has incorporated all different kinds of holidays to celebrate for many reasons. And she also gives great input for Publishing! I am happy to have this resource!"
Lee Ann Mancini, Author of *SeaKids Adventure Series* (animated cartoon) (2019 Edition)

Ginger Marks books are AMAZING! Her Marketing Guide is a MUST HAVE for those wanting to stand out in a crowd. All her books are wonderful. Ginger's Marketing Book is a PERFECT solution to all my sales & marketing needs. Don't miss out on her unique Marketing TIPS to think outside the box and stand out in a crowd. Thank you, Ginger Marks!
Jennifer P., Author/Illustrator (2019 Edition)

"Ginger Marks' Weird and Wacky Holiday Marketing Guide is a compendium of ideas to market your product, tying it to state, national and international celebrations of every conceivable kind. The research done for this book is mind-boggling. The holidays are organized by month, and list month-long, week-long and daily holidays. Appendix A provides a huge number of ready-made materials you can use for blog posts, flyers, press releases, etc. If you're looking to jump-start your marketing, you must get this book. Highly recommended."
—**A Writer (2018 Edition)**

"A Google Search on Steroids! Have you ever done a Google search while preparing a presentation and found an incredible list that helped you add lots of ideas to what you were doing? I have and know that having such a list always gives me lots of information to make my presentation more interesting and colorful.

"Ginger Marks' 2018 Weird & Wacky Holiday Marketing Guide is just like having the results of a Google search, only it is like having such a list on steroids! The guide contains an overwhelming number of marketing ideas. The first 70 pages list national, international, and quite frankly, often quirky and humorous events which take place throughout the year, listed in month-to-month order. If humor is what you are looking for, you will learn that National Hermit Week falls in June, "Hot Enough for Ya Day" falls on July 23rd, and August 7th is known as the "Particularly Preposterous Packaging Day." These three dates are just samples of the hundreds (even maybe a thousand) of weird and wacky celebrations, festivals, and events that are included in Ginger Marks' 2018 guide.

"The second half of the book contains several appendices, which once again provides all kinds of marketing information. I can't imagine a business owner who couldn't find some great marketing ideas while looking through the first half of this book, or who couldn't find links to companies that might help his or her business in the second half of the book. There is so much information here. The 2018 Weird & Wacky Holiday Marketing Guide is a terrific resource!"
Gary Ciesla (2018 Edition)

As someone who's taught "Marketing Your Biz on a Shoestring" for years, I always note the value of fun/crazy/unusual holidays for adding to your marketing options. Ginger has put together a great guide that gives you EVERYTHING: serious holidays, regularly scheduled holidays, and just for fun stuff.

—**Wendy Meyeroff, WM Medical Communications, Inc. (2018 Edition)**

"Ginger Marks has put together a fantastic resource! If you are looking for outside of the box ideas for marketing as well as for celebrating, you are going to love the Weird & Wacky Holiday Marketing Guide. As a former elementary school teacher, I wish I had had a copy of this incredible resource when I was teaching. The month-long and week-long holidays, listed throughout this guide, could create the foundation for exciting study units."

D'vorah Lansky, M.Ed. Best-Selling author of *Book Marketing Made Easy,* **www.BookMarketingMadeEasy.com (2016 Edition)**

"Great marketing tools for social media business exposure. Having multiple businesses and also doing websites, I found this book to be a wonderful asset for trying to come up with new "and different" ideas for marketing, especially on social media. Talk about having every holiday imaginable listed in this book!! There are also so many that it intrigues your interest to go off & further investigate on your own, after learning about them for the first time.

"I personally liked that at the end of the calendar month she adds some ideas on how to use these holidays to your advantage in marketing, but more importantly, she is always adding comments you can raise the money for charity or a good cause (not just to market your business but also help your community at the same time). If you have a business that is seeking attention on social media, I think this book will help you announce some totally Weird & Wacky facts for every day of the year, that will certainly get you noticed!! A wealth of resources here."

Cheryl (2018 Edition)

"So much info in one book! As a business owner, it's difficult to stand out. With Ginger's guidance you can set yourself apart from the crowd. It's well-written and easy to follow. Tons and tons of info and well worth it!"

Patti Knoles, Virtual Graphic Arts Department (2017 Edition)

"Awesome very practical and fun marketing ideas. Ginger Marks' 2018 Weird and Wacky Holiday Marketing Guide is an amazing book and tool for me to use preparing speeches in my business. Using anecdotes from the book I can enhance my presentations to be much more fun and colorful and keep the audience entertained. I can't wait to show this book to my colleagues.

"There are numerous marketing ideas I never would have come up with on my own that I plan to use in my business social media which should really help engagement. I love that I can get new ideas all year long!"

Rachel I (2018 Edition)

2020 Weird & Wacky Holiday Marketing Guide
12th Edition
Your business marketing calendar of ideas

Ginger Marks

DocUmeant *Publishing*
244 5th Avenue
Suite G-200
NY, NY 10001
646-233-4366
www.DocUmeantPublishing.com

Weird & Wacky Holiday Marketing Guide, Volume 12

Published by DocUmeant Publishing
244 5th Ave, Ste G–200
NY, NY 10001
646-233-4366

© Copyright 2020 Ginger Marks All rights reserved. No portion of this book may be duplicated in any way by any means, electronically or manually without the expressed written permission of the author, except for personal use. Address all comments and questions to Ginger.Marks@DocUmeantDesigns.com.

Editor Wendy VanHatten
VanHatten Writing Services
www.wendyvanhatten.com

Layout and Design Ginger Marks
DocUmeant Designs
www.DocUmeantDesigns.com

Library of Congress: 2019957976

ISBN: 978-1-950075-02-7 ($24.95)

Contents

Introduction -- 1

Annual Dates of Note -- 3
   United Nations International Year of Plant Health 3
   International Year of the Nurse and Midwife 3
   Chinese Year of the Rat 3
      Lucky Signs 3
      Strengths 4
      Weaknesses 4
      Best Jobs and Careers 4
      Matches 4
      Rat's Personality by Blood Type 4

JANUARY --- 5
   Month-Long Holidays 5
   Week-Long Holidays 5
   Daily Holidays 5
   Holiday Marketing Ideas 7

FEBRUARY --- 9
   Month-Long Holidays 9
   Week-Long Holidays 9
   Daily Holidays 9
   Holiday Marketing Ideas 11

MARCH --- 13
   Month-Long Holidays 13
   Week-Long Holidays 13
   Daily Holidays 14
   Holiday Marketing Ideas 16

APRIL --- 18
   Month-Long Holidays 18
   Week-Long Holidays 18
   Daily Holidays 19
   Holiday Marketing Ideas 21

MAY -- 23
   Month-Long Holidays 23
   Week-Long Holidays 23
   Daily Holidays 24
   Holiday Marketing Ideas 26

JUNE — 28
- State Fairs — 28
- Month-Long Holidays — 28
- Week-Long Holidays — 28
- Daily Holidays — 29
- Holiday Marketing Ideas — 30

JULY — 33
- State Fairs — 33
- Month-Long Holidays — 33
- Week-Long Holidays — 33
- Daily Holidays — 34
- Holiday Marketing Ideas — 35

AUGUST — 38
- State Fairs — 38
- Month-Long Holidays — 38
- Week-Long Holidays — 38
- Daily Holidays — 39
- Holiday Marketing Ideas — 41

SEPTEMBER — 43
- State Fairs — 43
- Month-Long Holidays — 43
- Week-Long Holidays — 43
- Daily Holidays — 44
- Holiday Marketing Ideas — 46

OCTOBER — 48
- State Fairs — 48
- Month-Long Holidays — 48
- Week-Long Holidays — 49
- Daily Holidays — 49
- Holiday Marketing Ideas — 51

NOVEMBER — 54
- Month-Long Holidays — 54
- Week-Long Holidays — 54
- Daily Holidays — 54
- Holiday Marketing Ideas — 56

DECEMBER — 59
- Month-Long Holidays — 59
- Week-Long Holidays — 59
- Daily Holidays — 59
- Holiday Marketing Ideas — 61

Appendix A: SAMPLES — 63
- Sample Press Release — 63
- Glaucoma Awareness Handout — 64

- Dragon Facts 65
  - Characteristics 65
  - Dragon Movie Titles 65
  - Dragon to Movie Match Game 65
- Birdseed Package 67
- Dracula Day Event Flyer 68
- Words Matter Week Card 69
- Words Matter Social Media Graphic 70
- World Poetry Day Graphic 71
- World Poetry Day Infographic 72
- Pony Express Game 73
- Chili Recipes 74
  - Best Damn Chili by Danny Jaye 74
  - Keith's White Chicken Chili 75
  - Michelle's Basic Chili 76
  - Holly's Best Chili Recipe 76
- Beaver Facts 77
- National High Five Day Graphic 78
- New Friends Old Friends Week Graphics 79
- Respect for Chickens Day Poster 81
- Respect for Chickens Day Button 82
- Sock Drive Flyer 83
- Towel Day Button 84
- How To Organize a Clothes Drive 85
- Upsy Daisy Day Graphic 87
- Asteroid Template 88
- Globe Template 89
- Sports Clichés* 93
  - Sports clichés used in business 93
  - Sports clichés used in sports announcing 93
  - Sports film clichés 94
  - References 95
- Sports Cliché Week Buttons 96
- National Watermelon Day Graphic 100
- Be an Angel Day Random Act of Kindness (RAK) Cards 101
- Fall Hat Month Social Media Graphic 102
- Fall Hat Month Clothing Drive 103
- Fall Hat Month Event Flyer 104
- List of Misused Words & Phrases 105
- 9x13 Day Graphic 106
- Tradesman Day Infographic 107
- Medical Records Organizational Tabs 108
- Wallet-Sized Medication Card 114
- Business Card-Sized Medication Card 115
- National Kick Butt Day Graphic 116
- International Evaluate Your Life Day Graphic 117
- Personal SWOT Analysis 118

Organ Donation Infographic.. 119
10 Ways to 'Loosen Up Lighten Up' Infographic 122
Be a Blessing Day Graphics 124
International Mountain Day Graphic 129

Appendix B: 2020 Social Media Image Size Guide — 130
Facebook.. 130
LinkedIn 130
YouTube 131
Instagram 131
Twitter.. 131
Pinterest 132
Tumbler 132
Google+ 132
Ello 133
SnapChat.. 133
Chinese Social Media 133
    WeChat 133
    Weibo 134

Appendix C: LINKS — 135
Link Checker 135
Article Marketing Sites 135
Auto Responder Services 135
Books and Movies.. 135
Greeting Card Companies 135
Podcast Directories.. 136
Promotional Product Supply Companies 136
Quote Sources... 137
Stock Photos 137
Teleconference Companies 138
Virtual Assistant Companies 138
Webinar Services 138

Appendix D: RESOURCES — 141

About the Author — 143

Additional Works by Ginger Marks — 145

Introduction

Events are one of the smartest prescriptions for slumping sales and for maintaining a healthy business. It's not enough anymore to merely have goods on the shelf and open the doors on time every day. We all need to reinvent our businesses to keep them thriving and healthy. And, that is just what this book helps you achieve.

This unique marketing book continues to win awards year after year and remains a #1 Best-Seller in the Business Marketing genre. Highly praised by marketing experts and now entering its second decade, this book offers more fun and easy marketing ideas exclusively penned for the calendar year 2020. Now you can grow your business with strategies built around wacky holidays, observed throughout the world, for the entire 2020 calendar year. If you missed the premier 2009 issue or want to complete your collection, all previous and unique yearly editions are available at http://www.HolidayMarketingGuide.com.

As *Weird & Wacky Holiday Marketing Guide* is read and used internationally, I have included many International holidays.

To take advantage of the information provided, pick a day and discover the unusual holidays celebrated on that date. Then, read the corresponding month's "Holiday Marketing Ideas" section to find a simple implementation or allow it to open your creative mind and think of some of your own.

Please note that the asterisk (*) in front of a holiday means a specific holiday is celebrated on that numerical date each year. For example, Christmas Day is December 25 no matter what day that falls on during the calendar week.

Here's another exceptional marketing idea for you I discovered when visiting BrownieLocks.com back in 2009, and which is now listed in the official *Chase Calendar of Events* which I cull from every year. Bonza Bottler Days™—the day is the same as the month it is in. That equates to: 1/1, 2/2, 3/3, etc. There is one in every month. There you have it; another extra fine excuse for an event to boost your notoriety and sales each and every month!

This is by no means a comprehensive edition. I have made all attempts to ensure the accuracy of the contents. If you encounter errors or know of a holiday that needs to be included, please let me know so they can be addressed in future editions. But remember, if your suggested holiday addition is not listed in the official *Chase Calendar of Events* it is not eligible for inclusion.

Read on, have fun, initiate your own version of these holidays, and reap the benefit for your business.

Ginger Marks

P.S. I have included a new section titled, "State Fairs" to simplify finding your state's fair.

P.S.S. The *Weird & Wacky Holiday Marketing Companion Playbook*. This tool is intended to help you to create, organize, and put the FUN back into your marketing plan. Each monthly calendar offers space for you to begin your planning and keep all your notes in one

handy book. Since each year the physical calendar days rotate, I have left the date numbers blank to enable you to make use of this *Companion Playbook* beginning today.

Annual Dates of Note

United Nations International Year of Plant Health

The International Year of Plant Health is a once in a lifetime opportunity to raise global awareness of the importance of plant health and how protecting plant health can help end hunger, reduce poverty, protect the environment, and boost economic development.

International Year of the Nurse and Midwife

For the first time in history, the nations of the world will unite in celebration of the benefits that nursing and midwifery bring to the health of the global population. It is being promoted by nursing and midwife organizations around the world. It is anchored on the 200th birth anniversary of modern nursing pioneer Florence Nightingale (1820–1910). The World Health Organization—the public health agency of the United Nations—has endorsed the year.

Chinese Year of the Rat[1]

Rat is the first in the 12-year cycle of Chinese zodiac. The Years of the Rat includes 1912, 1924, 1936, 1948, 1960, 1972, 1984, 1996, 2008, 2020, 2032 . . .

Though people consider the rat not adorable, and it even makes its way into derogatory languages, it ranks first on the Chinese zodiac signs. It has characteristics of an animal with spirit, wit, alertness, delicacy, flexibility, and vitality.

Lucky Signs

Lucky Numbers: 2, 3

Lucky Colors: gold, blue, green

Lucky Flowers: lily, African violet, lily of the valley

Lucky Directions: southeast, northeast

---

1 Travel China Guide. https://www.travelchinaguide.com/intro/social_customs/zodiac/rat.htm.

Strengths
Warm-hearted, good-tempered, loyal, honest, gentle

Weaknesses
Timid, unstable, stubborn, picky, lack of persistence, querulous

Best Jobs and Careers
Best Jobs: Artist, author, doctor, teacher
Best Working Partners: Ox, Monkey, Dragon
Best Age to Start a Business: 35–45
Best Career Fields: Service Industry, Finance and Economy Field

Matches
Perfect: Ox, Dragon, Monkey

They can get along with Ox, Dragon and Monkey partners, and their relationship will be well maintained as fresh as before. There is no big rise and fall in their lifetime, but there will never be a lack of romance and passion.

Avoid: Horse, Rooster

If they get together, there will be endless quarrels. They are all sharp in words, and seldom make compromises. Picky in each other's faults, they cannot be tolerant, which leads to their final divergence.

Rat's Personality by Blood Type

Blood Type O: They are positive, kind, and warm hearted. People admire their uprightness and principles.

Blood Type A: They are acute and thoughtful, for they can always sense the subtle changes of others. Tidy and orderly, they can always make the living place comfortable and cozy.

Blood Type B: Straightforward and outgoing in nature, they are faithful friends in others' eyes. Besides, they are loyal and persistent in relationships.

Blood Type AB: Humor and modesty are their shinning points, and for that they can make a lot of friends. They are assertive, having different insights in their own perspective.

JANUARY

Jan 6 – Feb 25 Carnival Season
Jan 7 – Feb 25 Germany: Munich Fasching Carnival
Jan 20 – Feb 19 Aquarius the Water Carrier
Jan 31 – Feb 17 Canada: Winterlude

Month-Long Holidays

Be Kind to Food Servers Month, Book Blitz Month, Children Impacted by a Parent's Cancer Month, Get Organized, International Child-Centered Divorce Month, International Creativity Month, National Clean Up Your Computer Month, National Glaucoma Awareness Month, National Hot Tea Month, National Mentoring Month, National Personal Self-Defense Awareness Month, National Poverty In America Awareness Month, National Radon Action Month, National Skating Month, National Slavery and Human Trafficking Prevention Month, National Volunteer Blood Donor Month, Oatmeal Month, Worldwide Rising Star Month

Week-Long Holidays

Jan 1 – 2 Taiwan: Foundation Days
Jan 2 – 8 Someday We'll Laugh About This Week
Jan 5 – 11 Dating and Life Coach Recognition Week
Jan 11 – 17 Cuckoo Dancing Week
Jan 18 – 19 Bald Eagle Appreciation Days
Jan 18 – 25 Week of Christian Unity
Jan 19 – 25 Snowcare for Troops Awareness Wee
Jan 26 – 31 Clean Out Your Inbox Week
Jan 26 – Feb 1 Catholic Schools Week

Daily Holidays

1. Betsy Ross Birthday (1752), *Bonza Bottler Day™, Canada: Polar Bear Swim 2020, *Copyright Revision Law Signed (1976), Cuba: Liberation Day, Czech-Slovak Divorce (1993), *Ellis Island Opened (1892), *Emancipation Proclamation Takes Effect (1863), *Euro Introduced (1999), *First Baby Boomer Born (1946), *Frankenstein (1818), *Haiti: Independence Day, *National Environmental Policy Act (50th Anniversary, 1970), *New Year's Day, *Paul Revere Birthday (1735),*Betsy Ross (1752), Russia New Year's Day Observance, Saint Basil's Day, Sudan: Independence Day, *Z Day
2. Isaac Asimov Birth (100th), 55-MPH Speed Limit (1974), Haiti: Ancestor's Day, *Happy Mew Year for Cats Day, Japan: Kakizome, Switzerland: Berchtoldstag, World Introvert Day
3. Congress Assembles, *Drinking Straw Day (1888), Memento Mori, JRR Tolkien Birth (1892)

4. *Amnesty for Polygamists (1893), *Dimpled Chad Day, *Myanmar: Independence Day, *Isaac Newton Birth (1643), *Pop Music Chart Introduced (1936), *Trivia Day, Utah: Admission Day, *World Braille Day, World's Tallest Building Dedicated (10th Anniversary, 2010)
5. *Alvin Ailey Birth (1931), Earth at Perihelion, *Five-Dollar-a-Day Minimum Wage Day (1914), National Bird Day, Twelfth Night
6. *Armenian Christmas, *Epiphany or Twelfth Day, National Thank God It's Monday Day, New Mexico Admission Day, *Three Kings Day
7. Asarah B'Tevet, *First Balloon Fight Across the English Channel (1785), *International Programmers' Day, Japan: Nanakusa, *National Bobblehead Day, Orthodox Christmas, Russia: Christmas Observed, TransAtlantic Phoning (1927)
8. Argyle Day, Greece: Midwife's Day or Women's Day, *National JoyGerm Day, *Show-and-Tell at Work Day, *War on Poverty (1964)
9. *Aviation in America (1793), *Panama: Martyrs' Day
10. League of Nations Founding (100th Anniversary, 1920), Lunar Eclipse, Women's Suffrage Amendment Introduced in Congress (1878)
11. Morocco: Independence Day, Nepal: National Unity Day, U.S. Surgeon Declares Cigarettes Hazardous (1964)
12. *Haiti Earthquake Day (2010), National Hot Tea Day, Switzerland: Meitlisunntic, Tanzania: Zanzibar Revolution Day
13. Japan: Coming-of-Age Day, National Clean-Off-Your-Desk Day, Norway: Tyvendedagen, *Radio Broadcasting Day (1910), Russian Old New Year's Eve, Sweden: St. Knut's Day, Togo: Liberation Day
14. *Arnold Benedict Day, Poetry at Work Day, *Ratification Day, Uzbekistan: Army Day
15. *Alpha Kappa Alpha Sorority Day, National Begel Day, Quarterly Estimated Federal Income Tax Day (also Apr 15, Jun 15, and Sep 15), Train for Paris Day (75th Anniversary, 1950)
16. *Appreciate a Dragon Day, *Civil Service Day, El Salvador: National Day of Peace, Get to know Your Customer Day (also Apr 16, Jul 16, and Oct 15), Japan Haru-No-Yabuiri, Malawi: John Chilembwe Day, National Nothing Day, National Quinoa Day, *Religious Freedom Day
17. Arbor Day in Florida, *Al Capone Day, *Ben Franklin Birthday (1706), Brontë 200 Day, *Cable Car Day, *Ben Franklin Day, International Fetish Day, *Judgment Day, Kid Inventors' Day, Lee-Jackson Day in Virginia, Mexico: Blessing of the Animals at the Cathedral, Poland: Liberation Day, Popeye Day, Saint Anthony's Day, Southern California Earthquake Day (1994), The Business of America Day (200th Anniversary, 1820)
18. National Use Your Gift Card Day, *Pooh Day
19. *Confederate Heroes Day in Texas, Ethiopia: Timket, Robert E. Lee Day, National Popcorn Day, Edgar Allen Poe Day, Stephen Foster Day
20. Azerbaijan: Martyrs' Day, Brazil: San Sebastian's Day, Guinea-Bissau: National Heroes Day, Martin Luther King, Jr Birth Observed (1986), Lesotho: Army Day, US Hostages in Iran Released (1091), US Revolutionary War Ends Day (1783)
21. Fist Supersonic Concorde Flight (1976), Kiwanis International Founding (1915), National Hug Your Puppy Day, *National Hugging Day
22. *Answer Your Cat's Question Day, Laugh-In Day, *Roe vs. Wade Decision (1973), *Saint Vincent: Feast DayUkraine: Ukrainian Day
23. Bulgaria: Babin Den (Midwives/Grandmother's Day), *National Handwriting Day, National Pie Day, Snowplow Mailbox Hockey Day

24. *Belly Laugh Day, California Gold Discovery Day, *Beer Can Day (1935), *National Compliment Day, United Nations: International Day of Education
25. *Around the World in 72 Days (1890), Chinese New Year, Local Quilt Shop Day, *Macintosh Debuts (1984), National Seed Swap Day, *A Room of One's Own Day, Saint Dwynwen's Day
26. Australia: Australia Day, Dental Drill Day, Dominican Republic: National Holiday, India: Republic Day, Indian Earthquake (2001), 2020 Pro Bowl, World Leprosy Day
27. Bubble Wrap® Appreciation Day, Canadian Caper/Operation Argo (40th Anniversary, 1980), Germany: Day of Remembrance for Victims of Nazism, Leningrad Liberated (1944), *Mozart Day, National Geographic Society Founded (1888) *Thomas Crapper Day, United Kingdom: Holocaust Memorial Day, United Nations: International Day of Commemoration in Memory of the Victims of the Holocaust, *Vietnam Peace Day
28. *Challenger Space Shuttle Explosion (1986), Data Privacy Day, Israeli Siege of Suez City Ends (1974), Scotland: Up Helly AA
29. *Curmdgeons Day, *Seeing Eye Dog Day
30. Inane Answering Message Day, National Croissant Day
31. *First Social Security Check Issued (8th Anniversary, 2012), *Inspire Your Heart with the Arts Day, National Preschool Fitness Day, Nauru: National Holiday

Holiday Marketing Ideas

National Glaucoma Awareness Month — Where would we be without good vision? Those who suffer from this disease know the impact the loss of vision can have on your business and your life. Let your care of the community show this month. Some of the ways you could promote your business while celebrating this month-long holiday are easy, while others will take a bit more patience and planning. Start with a simple card or social media blitz or consider raising awareness through events or a fundraiser. You might even partner with a local eye doctor in your area and do radio announcements if you are up to the challenge. Either way, you are sure to get noticed for your simple act of kindness. You'll find a card to get you started in Appendix A.

Jan 7 National Bobblehead Day — Do you know anyone who has ever had one of these in their car? If you do, or perhaps you are the guilty party, then you'll enjoy the celebration of this totally Weird & Wacky holiday. To celebrate on social media, you could share photos of favorite bobbleheads. Here's a hashtag that you should use, #NationalBobbleheadDay. Also, on Facebook, Twitter, and Instagram use @BobbleheadHall since they are the culprit who initiated this strange holiday. Why not host a bobblehead scavenger hunt? That could be fun and easy to do, and, it would help you get your fans to migrate through your entire website. Be sure to wish all your friends and fans a joyous National Bobblehead Day!

Jan 14 Ratification Day — Today is the perfect day to come to agreement with yourself and others. If you have been toying with the idea of a joint venture with another like-minded business owner, why not make this the day to get 'er done? As you grow your business, you'll find that you can't do it all yourself. So, the perfect solution is to enter into an agreement with someone who can do the task you can't or don't really enjoy doing.

Photo by Anthony Acosta from Pexels

To make this a marketing opportunity, hold your own 'summit' and invite others who are looking to grow their businesses. Let each owner talk about what they do and their needs. When you host an event like this your business will get noticed and you'll grow your goodwill and possibly your business as well.

Jan 16 Appreciate a Dragon Day— Let your inner child loose today. It's Appreciate a Dragon Day, and that's just what you want to focus on as you celebrate. One sure way to get your business noticed today is to share your dragon artwork or story if you are an artist or author. Why not consider hosting a reading event at your local library or bookstore? You might even want to try your hand at a grow your story event where each person gets to add a line to the tale.

However, if you aren't into art or writing, you can still participate by sharing dragon words of advice on social media. There are plenty of stories to cull from including *Pete's Dragon* or Draco. Or, how about sharing some dragon facts? To get you started there's a short list of interesting tidbits you can share and a list of dragons and their movies to help you in creating your own Dragon /Movie Match game in Appendix A.

Jan 24 National Compliment Day— What a wonderful opportunity to let your customers know how much you appreciate them! Spend the day sending out emails to your customers telling them one thing about them that you most appreciate. Better yet, send a note card. If you don't already have a fan or customer base, you might consider handing out slips of paper with compliments on them to those you come in contact with today. Don't forget to add your logo and contact data to get your name in their hands.

FEBRUARY

Feb 26 – Apr 11 Lent
Feb 28 – Mar 1 Chicago Comic & Entertainment Expo (C2E2)

Month-Long Holidays

African American Cultural Heritage Month, AMD/Low Vision Awareness Month, *American Heart Month, Feline Fix By Five Month, Library Lovers' Month, Marfan Syndrome Awareness Month, *National African American History Month, National Bird-Feeding Month, National Black History Month, National Cherry Month, National Condom Month, National Goat Yoga Month, National Parent Leadership Month®, National Pet Dental Health Month, National Time Management Month, Plant the Seeds of Greatness Month, Return Shopping Carts to the Supermarket Month, Spay/Neuter Awareness Month, Spunky Old Broads Month, Wise Health Care Consumer Month, Worldwide Renaissance of the Heart Month, Youth Leadership Month

Week-Long Holidays

Feb 2 – 8 African Heritage and Health Week
Feb 2 – 8 Dump your "Significant Jerk" Week
Feb 8 – 14 Love May Make the World Go 'Round, But Laughter Keeps us from Getting Dizzy Week
Feb 9 – 15 International Flirting Week, Love a Mensch Week
Feb 10 – 15 Freelance Writers Appreciation Week
Feb 11 – 13 World AG Expo
Feb 16 – 22 Build a Better Trade Show Image Week, National Engineers Week
Feb 23 – 25 Shrovetide
Feb 24 – 24 Germany & Austria: Fasching

Daily Holidays

1. *Betsy Ross Birthday (1752), Car Insurance Day, Freedom Day, G.I. Joe Day, Greensboro Sit-In (60th Anniversary, 1960), National Candy Making Day, *Robinson Crusoe Day, St. Laurent, Louis Stephen Day, Space Shuttle *Columbia* Disaster (2003), Take Your Child to the Library Day
1. *Bonza Bottler Day™, *Candlemas Day or Presentation of the Lord, *Groundhog Day, Hedgehog Day, *Imbolc, Luxembourg: Candlemas, Mexico: Dia de la Candelaria, *The Record of a Sneeze" (1893), Sled Dogs Save Nome (95th Anniversary, 1925), Switzerland: Homstrom
2. Abraham Lincoln Birthday Observed, *Four Chaplains Memorial Day, *Income Tax Birthday, Mozambiue: Heroes' Day, *"The Day the Music Died" (1959), Vietnam: National Holiday

3. African American Coaches Day, Angola: Armed Struggle Day, Apache Wars Begin (1868), *Facebook Launches (2004), Medjool Date Day, *Rosa Parks Birthday (1913), Sri Lanka: Independence Day, *USO Founded (1941), World Cancer Day
4. *Family Leave Bill Signing (1993), Longest War in History Ends (35th Anniversary, 1985), Mexico: Constitution Day, National Girls and Women in Sports Day, National Signing Day, *Weatherperson's Day
5. New Zealand: Waitangi Day, "Babe" Ruth Birthday (125th Anniversary, 1895), United Nations: International Day of Zero Tolerance for Female Genital Mutilation
6. *Ballet Day, Bubble Gum Day, *Chaplin's "Tramp" Day (1914), *Charles Dickens (1812), Grenada: Independence Day, National Black HIV/AIDS Awareness Day, *Wave Your Fingers at Your Neighbor Day
7. *Boy Scouts of America Day (1910), Chinese New Year in Sand Francisco, Japan: Hari-Kuyo (Festival of Broken Needles), Slovenia: Culture Day
8. *Beatles Day (1964), *Ernest Tubb (1914), *Gypsy Rose Lee (1914), Lebanon: Saint Maron's Day, Man Day, National Pizza Day, Read in the Bathtub Day
9. *"All the News That's Fit to Print" Slogan (1897), *Charles Lamb (1775), *First Computer Chess Victory over Human (1996), *First WWII Medal of Honor (1942), Man Day, *Plimsoll Day, Treaty of Paris (1763), Tu B'Shvat, United Nations: World Pulses Day
10. Cameroon: Youth Day, Thomas Edison Birthday (1847), Extraterrestrial Culture Day, *First Woman Episcopal Bishop (1989), Get Out Your Guitar Day, Iran: Victory of Islamic Revolution, *Japan: National Foundation Day, *National Shut-In Visitation Day, *Pro Sports Wives Day, *Satisfied Staying Single Day, United Nations: International Day of Women and Girls in Science, *Thomas Alva Edison Birthday (1847), Vatican City: Independence Day, White Shirt Day
11. *Abraham Lincoln (1809) and Birthplace Cabin Wreath Laying Day, *Darwin Day, *Dracula Day, Myanmar: Union Day, NAACP Founded (1909), *Oglethorpe Day, *Safetpup® Birthday, Utah: Women Given the Vote (150th Anniversary, 1870)
12. Dresden Firebombing (75th Anniversary, 1945), *Employee Awareness Day, *First Magazine Published in America (1741), *Get a Different Name Day, National Wingman`s Day, World Radio Day
13. Arizona: Admission Day, *ENAIC Computer Introduced (1946), *Ferris Wheel Day, *First African American To Be Recorded on Vinyl (100th Anniversary, 1920), *First Presidential Photograph (1849), *League of Women Voters Formed (100th Anniversary, 1920), National Donor Day, Oregon: Admission Day (1859), Race Relations Day, *Saint Valentine`s Day, Space Milestone: 100th Space Walk (2001)
14. *Asteroid Near Miss Day, *Canada: Maple Leaf Flag Adopted (55th Anniversary, 1910), *Chelyabinsky Meteor Explosion (2013), *Galileo Galilei Birthday (1564), Love Reset Day, *Lupercalia, Remember the *Maine* Day (1898), *Serbia: National Day, *Susan B Anthony Birthday (200th Anniversary, 1820), World Pangolin Day
15. Daytona 500, Lithuania: Independence Day
16. Canada: Family Day (Selected Provinces), *League of United Latin American Citizens (LULAC) Founded (1927), *My Way Day, *National PTA Founders`Day (1897), Presidents`Day, Random Acts of Kindness Day, George Washington`s Birthday Observed
17. Cow Milked While Flying in an Airplane Day (90th Anniversary, 1930), Gambia: Independence Day, Nepal: National Democracy Day, George Peabody (225th Anniversary, 1795), *Pluto Discovery Day, (90th Anniversary, 1930)

18. *Japanese Internment (1942), *Knights of Pythias Founding (1864), *US Landing on Iwo Jima (75th Anniversary, 1945)
19. Closest Approach of a Comet to Earth (1491), Introduce a Girl to Engineering Day/Discovere Girls Day, *Northern Hemisphere Hoodie-Hoo Day, *United Nations: World Day for Social Justice
20. Bangladesh: Martyrs Day, *United Nations: International Mother Language Day, *Washington Monument Dedicated 91885)
21. Florida Acquired by US (1819), *George Washington`s Birthday (1732), Montgomery Boycott Arrests (1956), National Margarita Day, Saint Lucia: Independence Day
22. Brunei Darussalam: National Day, *Curling is Cool Day, Diesel Engine Day, First Cloning of an Adult Animal (1997), Guyana: Anniversary of Republic, *Iwo Jima Day (75th Anniversary, 1945), Japan: Birthday of the Emperor, Orthodix Meatfare Sunday, Single-Tasking Day
23. Estonia: Independence Day, Georgian Calendar Day, Iceland: Bun Day, Mexico: Flag Day, Shrove Monday
24. Clay Becomes Heavyweight Champ (1964), Iceland: Bursting Day, Kuwait: National Day, Mardi Gras (Fat Tuesday), Paczki Day, Shrove Tuesday, World Spay Day
25. Ash Wednesday, *FCC (Federal Communications Commission) created (1934), *For Pete's Sake Day, Grand Canyon National Park Established (1919), *Levi Strauss Day
26. Dominican Republic: Independence Day, International Polar Bear Day, National Chili Day
27. Floral Design Day, National Customized Wheel and Tire Day, *National Tooth Fairy Day, Shabbat Across American and Canada, Taiwan: 288 Memorial Day
28. Bachelors Day, International Underlings Day, Leap Year Day, Open that Bottle Night

Holiday Marketing Ideas

National Bird-Feeding Month — This month you can help our fine feathered friends by handing out small packages of bird seed to those passing by. Have your business card stapled to it, or better yet, the entire package is branded to your company. Spend some time at a local park to enjoy watching them actually use your offering. You'll find a birdseed packet and template in Appendix A that you can brand or design your very own.

If you want something even easier to initiate, post bird photos along with facts about them on your favorite social media sites. Make it fun, by opening it up to others to join you posting their photos. Alternatively, you might want to think about an event titled "Pecking Order" which you could help people put their time management skills in practice. Keep your thinking cap on and I'm sure you'll come up with some fun events to showcase your business this month.

Feb 7 Bubble Gum Day – Here's another Weird & Wacky holiday that you can blow bubbles at. Of course, you could see who can blow the biggest bubble, or fill a jar and have them guess how many pieces are contained within. These are some obvious choices. But, other than the most obvious why not host a webinar or seminar on the topic of expanding. There's expanding their marketing reach, how not to pop their marketing bubble, aka, blowing the sale, or any number of other bubble related subjects. If you really want to do something simple hand out bubble gum with your business card attached everywhere you go today.

Feb 12 Dracula Day — This is one that I personally used to showcase my business in 2017. It was a bonus idea that I shared previously. In case you didn't see it, or had the opportunity to

participate in my event you'll be drooling over this blood sucking holiday. Yes, you have it. That's the theme of the day, stop the bloodsuckers from stealing your business or happiness. You can go it alone or invite other successful business owners or coaches to join you. Whatever you decide to do, be sure to get the energy flowing promoting your business in plenty of time to make it a great success. Of course, I've shared my event flyer in Appendix A.

Feb 18 Cow Milked While Flying in an Airplane Day — Talk about a Weird & Wacky holiday, this one has to be one of the weirdest! To jump start your idea machine think about how uncomfortable that cow must have been to need to be milked en route. So, what uncomfortable situations can you help others solve? Are you a coach or do you have a product or service that would make other's lives easier? This holiday also celebrates accomplishing what others thought impossible and proving its value. There are several ways you could assist others while promoting your products or services. Why not share tips on social media that will help them along their way? If not tips, a webinar or seminar might be in order.

Feb 28 National Tooth Fairy Day — Today is a day to grant someone's wishes. Why not donate to a worthy cause. Host a fundraiser or give of your time or knowledge. One particularly good idea is to work with a senior citizens home to provide entertainment or activities that they would appreciate and enjoy. Small gifts to children in the Ronald McDonald house would also be a kind reminder that wishes can come true. If you decide to host a fundraiser, or gift giving for the latter, be sure to let the media know. They still do feel-good stories and why shouldn't this one be about you and your business?

MARCH

Mar 13 – Apr 15 Deaf History Month
Mar 2 – Apr 10 Orthodox Lent
Mar 13 – Apr 15 Deaf History Month
Mar 29 – Apr 4 Consider Christianity Week
Mar 29 – Apr 11 Passiontide
Mar 30 – Apr 2 Italy: Bologna Children's Book Fair
Mar 30 – Apr 5 Mule Day

Month-Long Holidays

Alport Syndrome Awareness Month, *American Red Cross Month, Clap 4 Health Month, Colorectal Cancer Education and Awareness Month, Credit Education Month, Employee Spirit Month, Humorists Are Artists Month (HAAM), International Black Women In Jazz Month, International Ideas Month, International Mirth Month, *Irish American Heritage Month, Music In Our Schools Month, National Clean Up Your IRS Act Month, National Colorectal Cancer Awareness Month, National Kidney Month, National Multiple Sclerosis Education and Awareness Month, National Nutrition Month®, National Peanut Month, National Umbrella Month, National Women's History Month, Optimism Month, Paws to Read Month, Play-the-Recorder Month, Poison Prevention Awareness Month, Red Cross Month, Save the Vaquita Month, Save Your Vision Month, Social Work Month, *Women's History Month, Workplace Eye Wellness Month, Worldwide Home Schooling Awareness Month, Youth Art Month

Week-Long Holidays

Mar 1 – 7 Celebrate You Name Week, National Cheerleading Week, Will Eisner Week, Words Matter Week
Mar 2 – 6 National School Breakfast Week
Mar 4 – 7 Association of Writers and Writing Programs Conference and Bookfair
Mar 6 – 8 Aldo Leopold Weekend, International Festival of Owls
Mar 8 – 14 Termite Awareness Week
Mar 10 – 12 London Book Fair
Mar 11 – 17 Turkey Vultures Return to the Living Sign
Mar 12 – 15 Emerald City Comic Con
Mar 13 – 15 Sherlock Holmes Weekend
Mar 15 – 21 National Animal Poison Prevention Week, National Poison Prevention Week, World Folk Tales and Fables Week
Mar 16 – 22 Brain Awareness Week, International Teach Music Week
Mar 16 – 23 United Kingdom: Shakespeare Week
Mar 21 – 22 Military Through the Ages

Mar 21 – 27 United Nations: Week of Solidarity with the Peoples Struggling Against Racism and Racial Discrimination
Mar 22 – 28 National Protocol Officers Week

Daily Holidays

1. Baby Sleep Day, Betsy Ross Birthday (1752), Bosnia and Herzegovina: Independence Day, Ralph Waldo Emerson Birthday (1914), *Iceland: Beer Day, Namesake Day, World Compliment Day, Zero Discrimination Day
2. Australia: Eight Hour Day or Labor Day, Ethiopia: Adwa Day, Fun Facts about Names Day, Guam: Discovery Day or Magellan Day, *Highway Numbers Day (95th Anniversary, 1925), *King Kong Day, NEA's Read Across America Day, Orthodox Green Monday, Texas Independence Day
3. Alexander Graham Bell Birthday (1847), *Bonza Bottler Day™, Bulgaria: Liberation Day, Hin-Mah-Too-Yah-Lat-Kekt Birthday (1840), International Ear Care Day, Japan: Hina Matsuri (Doll Festival), Malawi: Martyr's Day, National Anthem Day, Peace Corps Day, Simplify-Your-Life Day, Town Meeting Day, Unique Names Day, United Nations: World Wildlife Day, What if Cats and Dogs Had Opposable Thumbs Day, World Birth Defects Day
4. Discover What Your Name Means Day, National Backcountry Ski Day, *National Grammar Day, Old Inauguration Day
5. Crispus Attucks Day (250th Death Anniversary, 1770), Nametag Day, National Poutine Day, Saint Piran's Day, United Kingdom and Ireland: World Book Day
6. *Dred Scott day, Dress in Blue Day, Ghana: Independence Day, Middle Name Pride Day, National Day of Unplugging (6th–7th tentative), *Michelangelo (1475)
7. Genealogy Day
8. Check Your Batteries Day, Daylight Savings Begins, International (Working) Women's Day, National Proofreading Day, Syrian Arab Republic: Revolution Day, United Nations: International Women's Day, United States Income Tax Anniversary (1913)
9. *Barbie Day, Belize: Baron Bliss Day, National Napping Day, Panic Day, United Kingdom: Commonwealth Day
10. International Bagpipe Day, *Mario Day, National Women and Girls HIV/AIDS Awareness Day, Purim, *Salvation Army in the US (1880), *Telephone Invention (1876), *US Paper Money Issued (1862)
11. Bureau of Indian Affairs Established (1824), Dream 2020 Day, *Johnny Appleseed Day, Key Deer Awareness Day, Lithuania: Restitution of Independence Day, Registered Dietitian Nutritionist Day
12. *FDR's First Fireside Chat (1933), Gabon: National Day, *Girl Scouts of the USA (1912), Great Bilzzard of '88, Lesotho: Moshoeshe's Day, Mauritius: Independence Day, World Kidney Day
13. Blame Someone Else Day, *Earmuffs Day, Friday the Thirteenth, Good Samaritan Involvement Day, Holy See: National Day, National Open an Umbrella Indoors Day, Planet Uranus Discovery Day (1781)
14. *Albert Einstein Birthday (1879), International Fanny Pack Day, Moth-er Day, Pi Day, "10 Most Wanted List" Day (1950)
15. Belarus: Constitution Day, Brutus Day, Ides of March, International Day of Action for the Seals, Liberia: J.J. Roberts Day, National Vo Day, True Confessions Day

16. Australia: Canberra Day, *Black Press Day (1827), Curlew Day, Freedom of Information Day, Goddard Day, *Lips Appreciation Day, National Panda Day, National Quilting Day, No Selfies Day, US Military Academy Founded (1802)
17. *Campfire USA Day, Evacuation Day, Ireland: National Day, Saint Patrick's Day
18. Aruba: Flag Day, Diesel Day, Forgive Mom and Dad Day, *National Biodiesel Day
19. Absolutely Incredible Kid Day, Iran: National Day of Oil, Japan: Vernal Equinox Day, Ostara, Proposal Day® (also Sept 22), Saint Joseph's Day, Swallows Return to San Juan Capistrano Day, US Standard Time Act (100th Anniversary, 1920), *Wyatt Earp (1848)
20. Iranian New Year: (Noruz), Naw-Ruz, Snowman Burning, Tunisia: Independence Day, United Nations: French Language Day, *United Nations: International Day of Happiness, *Won't You Be My Neighbor Day
21. *Bach Day, *First Round-the-World Balloon Flight (1999), India: New Year's Day, Lesotho: National Tree Planting Day, Memory Day, Namibia: Independence Day, National Healthy Fats Day, National Quilting Day, Play the Recorder Day, Save the Florida Panther Day, South Africa: Human Rights Day, *Twitter Day, *United Nations: International Day for the Elimination of Racial Discrimination, United Nations: International Day of Forests, United Nations: International Nowruz Day, United Nations: World Poetry Day, Walk in the Sand Day, World Down Syndrome Day
22. As Young As You Feel Day, England: Mothering Sunday, *International Day of The Seal, *Louis L'Amour Day (1908), Laser Patented Day (1960), *National Goof-off Day, Puerto Rico: Emancipation Day, United Nations: World Day for Water (aka World Water Day)
23. Beat the Clock Day, "Big Bertha Paris Gun Day, *Liberty Day, National Puppy Day, National Tamale Day, *Near Miss Day, "OK" Day, Pakistan: Republic Day, *United Nations: World Meteorological Day
24. American Diabetes Association Alert Day, Argentina: National Day of Memory for Truth and Justice, Exxon Valdez Oil Spill (1989), *Houdini Day (1874), National Agriculture Day, Philippine Independence, *World Tuberculosis Day
25. *Bed In for Peace Day, *Greece: Independence Day: Little Red Wagon Day, Manatee Appreciation Day, Maryland Day, National Medal of Honor Day, *Old New Year's Day, Pecan Day, Tolkien Reading Day, United Nations: International Day of Remembrance of The Victims of Slavery and The Transatlantic, United Nations: International Day of Solidarity with Detained and Missing Staff Members, Whole Grain Sampling Day
26. Bangladesh: Independence Day, Camp David Accord Day, *Legal Assistants Day, Live Long and Prosper Day, *Make Up Your Own Holiday Day
27. Alaska: Earthquake (1964), *FDA Approves Viagra Day, Myanmar: Resistance Day, *Quirky Country Music Song Titles Day
28. Big Bang Day, Czech Republic: Teachers' Day, Earth Hour
29. *Canada: British North America Act (1867), Central African Republic: Boganda Day, Dow Jones Day, England: Care Sunday, European Union: Daylight Saving Time (begins), National Mom & Pop Business Owners day, *Niagara Falls Runs Dry (1848), Taiwan: Youth Day, Texas Loves Children Day
30. Anesthetic Day, *Doctors Day, Earth Hour, Grass is Always Browner on the Other Side of the Fence Day, International Laundry Folding Day, *Pencil Day, Seward's Day, Trinidad and Tobago: Spiritual/Shouter Baptist Liberation Day, Vincent Van Gogh Day (1853), World Bipolar Day
31. *Bunsen Burner Day, Cesar Chavez Day, *Eiffel Tower Day (1998), International Hug a Medievalist Day, *National "She's Funny That Way" Day, World Back-up Day

Holiday Marketing Ideas

International Mirth Month — Let your humor loose this month. Have some fun, play some games, and celebrate the gaiety of the season. To enjoy this Weird & Wacky month's celebration of mirth while promoting your business is going to mean having a whole lot of fun. So, start with hosting a joke contest. Set some ground rules so things don't get carried away too far, but don't make them so strict you won't have any participants.

Keep the fun coming with a seminar or webinar that teaches us how to destress our lives. Coaches and sellers of relaxation or meditation products will do well to take advantage of this special celebration.

Of course, there's always the option of simply posting on social media, but try to get a little more Weird & Wacky than that and you'll be laughing all the way to the bank.

Mar 1 – 7 Words Matter Week — Fitting well with the month's theme, this Weird & Wacky holiday reminds us that what you say (and how you say it) does matter. Speaking coaches, therapists, and editors are just a few business owners who should rally around this holiday week. If you find yourself outside of this group, why not host a seminar or webinar and invite those who do to share their expertise. Hosting events and even sponsoring them is a terrific way to promote your business. So, take the time necessary to prepare for your event and you'll have a slew of grateful business owners and friends who will thank you. Oh, and remember to tell a joke or two along the way.

If you aren't up to the task of hosting an event, you'll find a card you can customize and share either online or in person in Appendix A. There's also a simple button to use on your favorite social media there.

Mar 5 National Poutine Day — Who doesn't love a holiday that focuses on culinary delights? Do you know what Poutine is? I sure didn't until I looked it up. It turns out that Poutine is a dish that originated in Canada that consists of French fries, topped with cheese curds and brown gravy. Add some smoked meat for a nice twist. An interesting combination to be sure.

Today simply share your favorite recipe or tweet the day away wishing all your Canadian clients and customers a happy National Poutine Day.

Mar 8 Check Your Batteries Day — Personal safety is important to all of us. So today, be sure to remind all your clients and customers to follow this sage advice. If you want to take it up a notch, why not put together a panel of speakers who are knowledgeable on the subject of personal safety issues. If it's for the kids, you might want to invite Safety Pup to join your event. If it is a live event and adults are more your style, then a karate instructor might be a better choice.

Mar 9 National Napping Day — On the heels of personal safety comes a very important health issue. If you don't know it, getting the proper rest is one of the most important health issues. So, stress related products or services, authors, or coaches, will all do well to use this Weird & Wacky holiday to market their businesses. If you are looking for giveaways, mood rings might be an option you'll find well received. Improvements in alertness, productivity, and mood have all been shown to improve with proper rest.

If you are up for a bit of frivolity and have employees, why not all wear your PJ's to work today? If you don't have a physical address, then posting photos on social media in your favorite PJ's. Be sure to use #NationalNappingDay when you post on social media.

Mar 14 International Fanny Pack Day— Fanny packs are all about convenience and organization. So, these themes could be on your list of ways to celebrate today. But, if you want to know the truth of the matter, this day was created by Nick Yates after receiving a fruitcake and a fanny pack as gag gifts.

This Weird & Wacky holiday came out of a random encounter he had with a homeless man who teased him about his fanny pack and so he gave him his fruitcake. This got him to thinking about feeding the homeless. And so, International Fanny Pack Day is about feeding the homeless while wearing fanny packs.

If you decide to focus your energy in this direction, strap on your fanny pack and organize your own food drive to help food pantries in your area. A shockingly large percentage of people who are hungry are children. Oh, and be sure you let the media know about your efforts. They'll be sure to want to share on their broadcast what you are doing to aid the community.

If you need help figuring out how to organize your food drive, you're in luck. On page 118 of the 2012 edition of this handy *Weird & Wacky Holiday Marketing Guide* you'll find all the information on how to set-up and run your own food drive. It is followed by a food drive list that you may find helpful. However, if you aren't lucky enough to own a copy of that edition you it's still available for purchase on Amazon or at www.HolidayMarketingGuide.com.

Mar 21 United Nations: World Poetry Day— Here's one for the poet in you. Start off a poem and have others contribute a line, see where it goes, and you'll do fine. If poetry isn't your bag, let your mind wander. For once you get started, you're sure to create stir, and others will want to jump in and share the fun of creating their own version of prose. At the very least share a line or two from your favorite poet. Simply sharing your prose on social media can be fun but be sure to add some style to it along with your logo as you wish the reader a very happy United Nations: World Poetry Day. You'll find one I created in Appendix A if you are at a loss for words. You are free to brand and share or use as inspiration to create your own. There are several different types of poetry, so you'll quickly see that poems don't have to rhyme. They can be Haiku, free verse, Cinquains, Epic poems, Ballads, Acrostics, or Sonnets. I have created an infographic that explains the differences. or it might be fun to share in bite size pieces on your favorite social media site.

Mar 26 Make Up Your Own Holiday Day— For those who can't find a single Weird & Wacky holiday to gear their marketing around this one is just for you. Make up your own, one that fits your needs and your audience. Make it something fun and frivolous and you'll be sure to capture your audience's attention. No matter what you come up with, your business will benefit and so will you.

APRIL

Apr 1 – May 10 National Card and Letter Writing Month
Apr 7 – 20 Passiontide
Apr 24 – May 23 Ramadan: the Islamic Month of Fasting

Month-Long Holidays

Adopt a Ferret Month, Distracted Driving Awareness Month, Community Spirit Days, Global Astronomy Month, Grange Month, Holy Humor Month, Informed Woman Month, International Black Women's History Month, International Customer Loyalty Month, International Twit Award Month, Jazz Appreciation Month, Library Snapshot Day, Mathematics and Statistics Awareness Month, Medical Cannabis Education and Awareness Month, National African American Women's Fitness Month, National Autism Awareness Month, *National Cancer Control Month, *National Child Abuse Prevention Month, National Child Abuse Prevention Month, *National Donate Life Month, National Exchange Club Child Abuse Prevention Month, National Frog Month, National Heartworm Awareness Month, National Humor Month, National Lawn Care Month, National 9-1-1 Education Month, National Occupational Therapy Month, National Pecan Month, National Pest Management Month, National Poetry Month, National Rebuilding Month, *National Sexual Assault Awareness and Prevention Month, National Sexually Transmitted Diseases (STDS) Education and Awareness Month, National Youth Sports Safety Month, Pet First Aid Awareness Month, Pharmacists' War On Diabetes, Prevention of Cruelty to Animals Month, Rosacea Awareness Month, School Library Month, Straw Hat Month, Stress Awareness Month, Women's Eye Health and Safety Month, Workplace Conflict Awareness Month, World Landscape Architecture Month, Worldwide Bereaved Spouses Awareness Month

Week-Long Holidays

Apr 1 – 7 Laugh at Work Week
Apr 2 – 5 French Quarter Festival
Apr 4 – 10 Hate Week — "Down with Big Brother"
Apr 4 – 12 National Robotics Week
Apr 5 – 11 Greece: Dumb Week, Pan American Week, Holy Week, Philippines: Holy Week
Apr 6 – 10 Explore Your Career Options Week
April 9 – 16 Pesach or Passover
Apr 12 – 18 National Dog Bite Prevention Week, Orthodox Holy Week, Pan American Week
Apr 18 – 19 Just Pray No! Worldwide Weekend of Prayer and Fasting
Apr 18 – 26 National Park Week (tentative)
Apr 19 – 25 Chemists Celebrate Earth Week, National Coin Week, National Crime Victims' Rights Week, National Library Week, National Volunteer Week
Apr 23 – 26 Fiddler's Frolics
Apr 20 – 24 Administrative Professionals Week, Undergraduate Research Week
Apr 24 – 30 World Immunization Week

Apr 26 – May 2 Preservation Week
Apr 26 – May 3 Stewardship Week

Daily Holidays

1. *April Fool's or All Fool's Day, Bulgaria: St Lasarus' Day, Canada: Nunavut Independence (1999), Iran: Islamic Republic Day, Mule Day, *Sorry Charlie Day, US Air Force Academy Day
2. Hans Christian Anderson Day (1805), Argentina: Malvinas Day, *Sir Alec Guinness (1914), Love Your Produce Manager Day, National Ferret Day, Pascua Day, Ponce de Leon Discovers Florida (1513), *Reconciliation Day, *United Nations: World Autism Awareness Day, US Mint Day
3. Blacks Ruled Eligible to Vote Day (1944), Guinea: Anniversary of the Second Republic, *Pony Express Day, International Kids' Yoga Day, Taiwan: Children's Day, *Tweed Day
4. *Beatles Take Over Music Charts (1964), *Bonza Bottler Day™, Flag Act of 1818 Day, International Pillow Fight Day, Maya Angelou Birthday (1928), Senegal: Independence Day, *United Nations: International Day for Mine Awareness and Assistance in Mine Action, *Vitamin C Day
5. Education Sharing Day, Gold Star Spouses Day, National Deep Dish Pizza Day, Palm Sunday
6. Drowsy Driver Awareness Day, North Pole Discovery Day, *Tartan Day, *Teflon Day (1938), Thailand: Chakri Day, United Nations: International Day of Sport for Development and Peace
7. *International Beaver Day, International Snailpapers Day, *Metric System Day, National Beer Day (1933), National Making the First Move Day, *No Housework Day, United Nations: International Day of the Reflection on the Genocide in Rwanda, *United Nations: World Health Day
8. Home Run Record Set by Hank Aaron (1974), International Roma Day, Japan: Flower Festival (Hana Matsuri), National Dog Fighting Awareness Day, Passover (begins at sundown)
9. *Civil Rights Bill of 1866 Day, Civil War Ends (1865), *Jenkins Ear Day, Jumbo the Elephant Day, Maundy Thursday or Holy Thursday, National Former Prisoner of War Recognition Day, Philippines: Araw Ng Kagitingan, Texas Panhandle Tornado Day, Tunisia: Martyrs' Day, *Winston Churchill Day
10. ASPCA Incorporation Day (1866), Bermuda: Good Friday Kite Flying Day, *Commodore Perry Day, Good Friday, *National Siblings Day, *Salvation Army Founder's Day
11. *Barbershop Quartet Day, Civil Rights Act Day (1968), Costa Rica: Juan Santamaria Day, Easter Even *International "Louie Louie" Day, Lazarus Saturday, National Catch and Release Day, National Pet Day, Uganda: Liberation Day, World Parkinson's Day
12. Easter Sunday, Halifax: Independence Day, *National D.E.A.R. Day (aka Drop Everything and Read), *National Licorice Day, Orthodox Palm Sunday, Polio Vaccine Day, Truancy Day, United Nations: International Day of Human Space Flight, *Walk on Your Wild Side Day, Yuri's Night
13. Dyngus Day USA, Easter Monday, *Guy Fawkes Day, South Africa: Family Day, Sri Lanka: Sinhala and Tamil New Year, *Thomas Jefferson Day
14. *Children with Alopecia Day, Children's Day in Florida (always the second Tuesday), Dictionary Day, International Be Kind to Lawyers Day, *International Moment of Laughter Day, Pan American Day, Pathologists' Assistant Day

15. Astronomers Find New Solar System (1999), 123rd Boston Marathon and Bombing (2013), Botox Day, First School for Deaf Founded (1817), *Income Tax Pay Day, *McDonald's Day, *National Take a Wild Guess Day, *National That Sucks Day, Quarterly Estimated Federal Income Tax Payers' Due Date (also Jan 15, Jun 15, and Sep 15, 2020), *Titanic Sinking (1912)
16. *Charlie Chaplin Day (1889), Emancipation Day, Get to Know Your Customers Day (third Thursday of each quarter is set aside to get to know your customers even better), National High Five Day, National Stress Awareness Day
17. American Samoa: Flag Day, *Blah! Blah! Blah! Day, Herbalist Day, International Haiku Poetry Day, Syrian Arab Republic: Independence Day
18. America's Oldest Brewery Day (1829), Canada: Constitution Act of 1982, International Raw Milk Cheese Appreciation Day, *International Amateur Radio Day, Paul Revere's Ride Day (1775), *Pet Owners Independence Day, Record Store Day, "Third World" Day, World Circus Day, World Heritage Day/International Day for Monuments and Sites, Zimbabwe: Independence Day
19. John Parker Day, National Hanging Out Day, Orthodox Easter Sunday or Pascha, Patriots Day in Florida, Sierra Leone: National Holiday, Swaziland: King's Birthday, Uruguay: Landing of the 33 Patriots Day
20. Boston Marathon, 4/20 Day, Patriots Day in Massachusetts and Maine, United Nations: Chinese Language Day
21. Aggie Muster Day, Brazil: Tiradentes Day, India: Vaisakhi, Indonesia: Kartini day, Isreal: Yom Hashoah, Italy: Birthday of Rome, *Kindergarten Day, National Bulldogs are Beautiful Day, National Library Workers Day, Red Baron Day, San Jacinto Day
22. Administrative Professionals Day or Secretary's Day, Brazil: Discovery of Brazil Day, Coins Stamped "In God We Trust" Day, *Earth Day, Brazil Day, National Book Mobile Day, *National Jelly Bean Day, Oklahoma Land Rush Day (1889), United Nations: International Mother Earth Day
23. Canada: Newfoundland: Saint George's Day, *Movie Theatre Day, *Public School Day, National English Muffin Day, Saint George Feast Day, Spain: Book Day and Lover's Day, Turkey: National Sovereignty and Children's Day, William Shakespeare Day (1564), Spain: Book Day and Lover's Day, Take Our Daughters and Sons to Work® Day (fourth Thursday in April), Turkey: National Sovereignty and Children's Day, United Nations: English Language Day, United Nations: Spanish Language Day, *United Nations: World Book and Copyright Day, World Book Night
24. Armenia: Armenian Martyrs Day, Ireland: Easter Rising (1916), Library of Congress Day, National Arbor Day, National Arbor Day, National Hairball Awareness Day, National Teach Children to Save Day
25. Abortion Legalized (1967), Anzac Day, Egypt: Sinai Day, *License Plates Day, Independent Bookstore Day, Italy: Liberation Day, National Dance Day, National Rebuilding Day, Pet Tech CPR Day, Portugal: Liberty Day, Swaziland: National Flag Day, World Healing Day, World Malaria Day, World Penguin Day, World Tai Chi and Qigong Day, World Veterinary Day, WWII: East Meets West Day (75th Anniversary, 1945)
26. Audubon Day, Florida and Georgia: Confederate Memorial Day, *Hug an Australian Day, National Help a Horse Day, National Pretzel Day, *Richter Scale Day, Switzerland: Landsgemeinde, Tanzania: Union Day, United Nations: International Chernobyl Disaster Remembrance Day, United Nations: World Intellectual Property Day
27. Alabama & Mississippi: Confederate Memorial Day, *Babe Ruth Day (1947), Mantanzas Mule Day, *Morse Code Day, Most Tornadoes in a Day (US), Most Tornadoes in a

Day Day, National Little Pampered Dog Day, Netherlands: King's Day, Sierra Leon and Togo: Independence Day, Slovenia: Insurrection Day, South Africa, Freedom Day, World Healing Day
28. Biological Clock Gene Discovered (1994), Canada: National Day of Mourning, Israel: Yom Ha'zikkaron, United Nations: World Day for Safety and Health at Work, Workers Memorial Day
29. Emperor Hirohito Michi-No-Miya Birthday (1901), Isreal: Independence Day, Japan: Showa Day, *"Peace" Rose Day, Zipper Day (1913)
30. Beltane, *Bugs Bunny Day (1938), China: Birthday of Lord Buddha, Día de los Niños/Día de los Libros, First North America Theatrical Performance Day (1598), International Jazz Day, Louisiana Purchase Day (1803), National Animal Advocacy Day, National Honesty Day (Honest Abe Awards), Raisin Day, Organization of American States Founded (1948), Vietnam: Liberation Day, *Walpurgis Night

Holiday Marketing Ideas

International Twit Award Month — Let the shenanigans begin! This month we are going to have a bit of frivolity as we point to the twits among us. If you've ever done something totally stupid — raising my own hand — then you are officially a Twit. A fun way to celebrate would be to have others post the most inane thing they ever have done, and then award some gag gifts for the winners. We all know how events help us get our name out there, and when we do, people will remember us in their time of need. Add to that a bit of mirth and you have a winning combination.

Apr 3 Pony Express Day — Mail delivery used to take months and required hardy men to ride long and hard across dangerous territory to deliver it. That was eons ago. With the advancement in technology today our messages are delivered almost instantaneously. Are we spoiled or what?

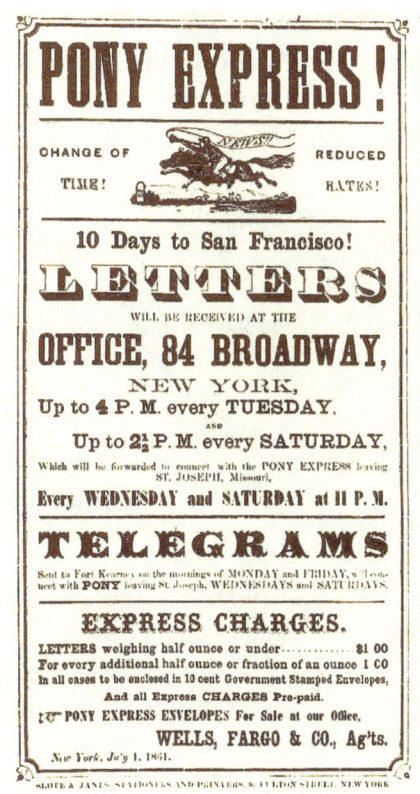

This is one of those holidays that is always on the same day every year, so it must be a biggie. So, let's think of a way we can market our businesses while recalling bygone days. Social media posts are the easiest way to celebrate today, but you might want to go a bit further. Don your best pony express rider attire and snap a photo to share or wear it all day long. Or, since chili was one of the early rider staples, why not host a chili cook off or recipe swap. There are lots of varieties of chili from beef and beans to chicken. You'll find a few in Appendix A if you want to try your hand at cooking up a batch to share with the homeless. Now there's an idea that is sure to get the media's attention, eh?

At your event you will want to be sure to play the Pony Express game. I've placed the instructions and the resource in the appropriate appendices for your convenience.

Apr 6 Teflon Day — To me Teflon is all about healthier cooking without so much oil and easier clean-up. So, immediately I think of businesses who teach you to live a healthier life and also those who help make our lives a bit easier.

With this thought in mind cooking classes, nutritionists, and even fitness experts should consider this a wonderful opportunity to market their businesses. Tweets, tips, and small token gifts with their business card attached will get you started, and events and seminars will be most beneficial.

Then we have those who make our lives easier. Stress reduction products and services, Virtual Assistants, phone answering services, and even candle sellers fit that bill. Be ready to share your expertise and services with tips and tricks to make other's lives easier.

Apr 7 International Beaver Day — Beavers are important to the environment. This is one reason they deserve their day in the sun. As we look to celebrating the impact they have on our planet we should focus on what we can do to bring awareness to the conservation of their habitat. Whether you decide to participate in or organize a coastal clean-up or other environmentally friendly adventure or take some children for a hike you're sure to enjoy celebrating this day in the wonderful world of beavers.

If you aren't up to an event such as this but still want to spend the day bringing awareness to your community, share the information you find online or in your local library about beavers. I have designed a piece you can print and share or post on your social media sites. If you wish to you might share the facts you will find on it as tips throughout the day. The hashtag for this special holiday is #BeaverDay in case you want to know.

In my search about this Weird & Wacky holiday I discovered a website that will send you a free PowerPoint presentation you can share if you let them know well before your event. You'll find the link to them in Appendix D.

Apr 16 National High Five Day — #NH5D is the hashtag to use today. It's about giving high fives and spreading good vibes all day long. Post videos giving high fives today or go a bit further and host a fundraiser. Use the graphic you will find in Appendix A, if you like, and for every share you and your company or group can donate a specific amount to a worthy cause. I can guarantee that if you do that others will indeed join you. When you let the media know what you are going to do ahead of time, they'll be sure to want to cover the event with, at the very least, a mention of you and your company.

Apr 26 Richter Scale Day — Hold onto your hats! Today is Richter Scale Day. The Richter Scale is a barometer of seismology, which is the measurement of the magnitude of earthquakes. So, today is your chance to shake things up a bit. Some perfectly grand ideas to shake up your prospects are to offer life changing solutions in bite-sized chunks or in an earthshaking live event. Folks who focus on careers and career changes, as well as breaking bad habits all would do well to market their businesses today. Procrastination is a huge problem for many business owners. So, coaches of all kinds from health and fitness experts to marketing and stress related businesses could benefit from a marketing push today.

May 12 – 23 Cannes Film Festival
May 30 – Jul 14 Cricket World Cup

Month-Long Holidays

*Asian American and Pacific Islander Heritage Month, Asthma Awareness Month, Fibromyalgia Education and Awareness Month, Gardening for Wildlife Month, Get Caught Reading Month, Gifts From the Garden Month, Global Civility Awareness Month, Huntington's Disease Awareness Month, International Mediterranean Diet Month, International Victorious Woman Month, *Jewish American Heritage Month, Law Enforcement Appreciation Month In Florida, Mental Health Month, Motorcycle Safety Month, Mystery Month, National Allergy/Asthma Awareness Month, National Arthritis Awareness Month, National Barbecue Month, National Bike Month, National Foster Care Month, National Good Car-Keeping Month, National Hamburger Month, National Hepatitis Awareness Month, National Meditation Month, National Military Appreciation Month, National Osteoporosis Month, National Physical Fitness and Sports Month, National Preservation Month, National Read to Your Baby Bump Month, National Salad Month, National Vinegar Month, *Older Americans Month, React Month, Save Your Tooth Month, Skin Cancer Awareness Month, Spiritual Literacy Month, Strike Out Strokes Month, Ultraviolet Awareness Month, Women's Health Care Month, Young Achievers/Leaders of Tomorrow Month

Week-Long Holidays

May 1 – 7 Choose Privacy Week
May 3 – 9 Be Kind to Animals Week®, National Family Week, National Hug Holiday Week, National Hurricane Preparedness Week, National Small Business Week, Small Business Week, Update Your References Week
May 4 – 8 Teacher Appreciation Week
May 4 – 10 National Pet Week
May 6 – 12 National Nurses Week
May 10 – 16 National Police Week, National Transportation Week, Salute to 35+ Moms Week
May 11 – 15 National Etiquette Week
May 11 – 17 National Stuttering Awareness Week, Work at Home Moms Week
May 16 – 17 Fishing Has No Boundaries Days
May 16 – 21 National Foul Ball Week
May 16 – 22 National Safe Boating Week
May 17 – 23 International New Friends Old Friends Week, National Unicycle Week, World Trade Week
May 24 – 30 National African Violet Week
May 25 – Jun 1 National Backyard Games Week
May 27 – 29 Book Expo America
May 30 – 31 BookCon 2020

Daily Holidays

1. *Amtrak, Batman Day, Batman Debut Anniversary (1939), Great Britain Formed Day (1707), Hug Your Cat Day, Skyscraper Day, *Keep Kids Alive — Drive 25® Day, Labor Day, *Law Day, *Lei Day, *Loyalty Day, *May Day, May One Day, Mother Goose Day, National Bubba Day, *New Home Owners Day, Russia: International Labor Day, *School Principals' Day
2. Free Comic Book Day, Kentucky Derby, King James Bible Published Day, Learn to Ride a Bike Day, National Auctioneers Day, National Fitness Day, Spring Astronomy Day, United Nations: World Tuna Day, Red Baron Day
3. Dow Jones Tops 11,000 Day (1999), *Garden Meditation Day, *Lumpy Rug Day, Mexico: Day of the Holy Cross, Motorcycle Mass and Blessing of the Bikes, National Infertility Survival® Day, National Public Radio Day, National Specially-Abled Pets Day, *National Two Different Colored Shoes Day, Poland: Constitution Day (Swieto Trzeciego Maja), *United Nations: World Press Freedom Day
4. China: Youth Day, Curaçao: Memorial Day, Jamaica Discover Day (1494), *International Respect for Chickens Day, Japan: Greenery Day, Melanoma Monday, Rhode Island: Independence Day, *Star Wars Day, United Kingdom: May Day
5. AMA Founded Day (1847), *Bonza Bottler Day™, *Cartoonists Day, *Cinco de Mayo, Ethiopia: Patriots Victory Day, International Day of the Midwife, Japan and South Korea: Children's Day, National Teacher Day, Netherlands: Liberation Day, World Asthma Day
6. International Management Accounting Day, Japan: Constitution Memorial Day Observed), *Joseph Brackett Day, National Bike to School Day, National School Nurses Day, *No Diet Day, *No Homework Day, Orson Wells Day (1915)
7. Beaufort Scale Day, Birthday of Buddha (Day of Vesak), Cystinosis Awareness Day, Dow Jones Tops 15000 (2013), El Salvador: Day of the Soldier, National Day of Prayer, National Day of Reason
8. Czech Republic: Liberation Day, Denmark: Common Prayer Day, England: Heston Furry dance/Flora Day, France: Victory Day, Military Spouse Appreciation Day, *No Socks Day, Slovakia: Liberation Day, *United Nations: Time of Remembrance and Reconciliation WWII (8–9), *V E Day (75th Anniversary, 1945), *World Red Cross Red Crescent Day
9. European Union Founded (1950), International Migratory Bird Day, Italy: Giro D'Italia, Jamestown Day, Letter Carriers' "Stamp Out Hunger" Food Drive, National Babysitters Day, Netherlands: National Windmill Day, Russia: Victory Day, Stay Up All Night Night, Uzbekistan: Day or Memory and Honor World Fair Trade Day
10. Golden Spike Driving Day (1758), Mother's Day, Mother's Day at the Wall, Taiwan: Birthday of Buddha, World Lupus Day
11. *Eat What You Want Day, United Nations: World Migratory Bird Day
12. *Limerick Day, Native American Rights Recognized Anniversary (1879), *Odometer Day
13. Children of Fallen Patriots Day, Donate a Day's Wages to Charity Day, National Hummus Day, National Nightshift Workers Day, National Receptionists Day
14. Fahrenheit Day, *Lewis and Clark Expedition Sets Out Day (1804), Smallpox Vaccine Discovery (1796), *The Stars and Stripes Forever Day, *Underground America Day, WAAC Day (1942)
15. Endangered Species Day, Fishing Has No Boundaries Day, Flight Attendant Day, International Learn to Swim Day, Japan: Aoi Matsuri (Hollyhock Festival), Mexico: San Isidro Day, Nakba Day, National Bike to Work Day, National Defense Transportation

Day, National Pizza Party Day, National Sliders Day, *Nylon Stockings Day, Paraguay: Independence Day, *Peace Officer Memorial Day, Teacher's Day in Florida, *United Nations: International Day of Families
16. Armed Forces Day, *Academy Awards Day (1929), *Biographer's Day, *First Woman to Climb Mt Everest Day (1975), Peabody Day, Preakness Stakes
17. Brown vs. Board of Education (1954), *First Kentucky Derby Day (1875), Ride a Unicycle Day, Rogation Sunday, Rural Live Sunday, *Same-Sex Marriages Day (2004), *United Nations: World Telecommunications and Information Society Day
18. Canada: Victoria Day, Haiti: Flag and University Day, *International Museum Day, Supply Chain Professionals Day, Uruguay: Battle of Las Piedras Day, *Visit Your Relatives Day
19. *Boys Club Day, Dark Day in New England, Hepatitis Testing Day, Ho Chi Minh Birthday (1890), Turkey: Youth and Sports Day
20. *Amelia Earhart Atlantic Crossing Day (1932), Cameroon: National Holiday, East Timor: Anniversary of Independence, *Eliza Doolittle Day, Lindbergh Flight (1927), Mecklenburg Day, *Weights and Measures Day, World Aiarthritis Day
21. *American Red Cross Founder's Day, Ascension Day, Chile: Battle of Iquique Day, *I Need a Patch for That Day, National Eat More Fruits and Vegetables Day, *National Wait Staff Day, *United Nations: World Day for Cultural Diversity for Dialogue and Development
22. Israel: Yom Yerushalayim, Mr. Rogers Neighborhood Day, *National Maritime Day, Sri Lanka: National Heroes Day, *United Nations: International Day for Biological Diversity, US Colored Troops Founders Day, World Goth Day, Yemen: National Day
23. *Bonnie and Clyde Death (1934), Declaration of the Bab, *International World Turtle Day®, Lag B'Omer, Morocco: National Day, National Best Friend-In-Law Day, New York Public Library Day, Sweden: Linnaeus Day, United Nations: International Day to End Obstetric Fistula
24. Belize: Commonwealth Day, Brooklyn Bridge Open (1883), *Brother's Day, Eritrea: Independence Day, International Tiara Day, *Morse Code Day
25. African Freedom Day, Argentina: Revolution Day, *Greatest Day in Track and Field: Jessie Owens' Day, *Ralph Waldo Emerson Birthday (1803), Jordan: Independence Day, Memorial Day, *National Missing Children's Day, *National Tap Dance Day, Poetry Day in Florida, Prayer for Peace Memorial Day, *Towel Day, United Nations: Week of Solidarity with Peoples of Non-Self-Governing Territories
26. Australia: Sorry Day, Georgia: Independence Day, John Wayne (1907), World Lindy Hop Day
27. *Cellophane Tape Day, First Flight into the Stratosphere (1931), First Running of the Preakness, *Golden Gate Bridge Day, World Otter Day
28. *Amnesty International Founded (1961), Ascension of Baha'u'llah, Azerbaijan: Day of the Republic, Ethiopia and Nepal: National Day, Orthodox Ascension Day, Shavout (begins at sundown), *Sierra Club Day, *Slugs Return from Capistrano Day
29. *Amnesty for Southern Rebels Day, *Mount Everest Summit Reached (1953), *United Nations: International Day of United Nations Peacekeepers
30. Ascension Day, Fabergé Day, *First American Daily Newspaper Published (1783), *Indianapolis 500 (1911), *Loomis Day, Memorial Day (Traditional)
31. *Copyright Law Passed (1970), Haiti: Mother's Day, Johnstown Flood Day, Pentecost, *United Nations: World No–Tobacco Day, *Walt Whitman Day, *What You Think Upon Grows Day, WhitSunday

Holiday Marketing Ideas

National Preservation Month—This month is set aside to honor the history all around us. From buildings to events all of history is worth preserving in knowledge and form. So to raise awareness of the historical sites near you lend a hand in events that promote historic places and demonstrate social and economic benefits they provide. When you participate in events such as these not only do you benefit the community, but you yourself will benefit as well.

Share photos of historic places that you have visited or would like to visit. Post them on social media websites and share a little history about them. Be sure to at least use #NationalRegister and #historicpreservation when posting on social media.

May 17–23 International New Friends Old Friends Week—What a great holiday to share your love for your closest pals and to make new ones. The absolutely best way to do that is to get out of your comfort zone and reach out to someone you've been wanting to get to know. Hosting an event, either online or live can open up new experiences and acquaintances as well as reminding us who our closest allies are. With a whole week to celebrate you are sure to make at least a few new friends and perhaps even renew old ones.

To get you started in celebrating, you'll find a graphic I designed in Appendix A promoting this Weird & Wacky holiday. Don't forget to brand it to your business. If you need help doing so, let me know, I'll be happy to assist you in your endeavor, or we can even create something special just for you.

May 4 International Respect for Chickens Day—Today is about standing up for the bleak conditions of poultry. However, they aren't the only ones who suffer. Families right here in our own country can be found who need our help. So, today is a day to do something about it. Not only for the chickens but for the children as well. Fundraising or a food or clothing drive might be a good start. There are always social media posts and such to get the word out. Be sure to brand your pics that you post so others who pass them on will share them and will pass on your business info too. You'll find a button you can share and a flyer too that you can brand to your business in Appendix A.

May 8 No Socks Day—My first thought is a sock drive! Many school age children don't have clean undergarments to wear. In my community we have a clothes for kids program that we give to annually. Why not start one in your community today or if you have one sponsor a sock drive to help? Oh, and don't forget, take 'em off! Wiggle those toes. It is No Socks Day after all.

Don't know how to put together a "drive"? Grab your 2012 edition of Weird & Wacky Guide and you'll find everything you need to know. While it relates to a food drive, the principle is the same. However, if you don't happen to already own it, you can still find it available for sale at http://www.HolidayMarketingGuide.com. If you wish you can use the flyer to promote your sock drive that you will find in Appendix A. While I'm at it, I'll just put the instructions for setting up a clothes drive in there too.

May 15 National Pizza Party Day—Do I hear a collective, "YUMMM!"? Whether you have a virtual or live pizza party everyone is sure to enjoy. Here's an idea for you. Share your favorite recipe or share memories about a memorable time when sitting around eating pizza. Or just wish everyone a happy National Pizza Party Day. If you are a philanthropist in nature you could either work with a local pizza palace and hand out coupons for a slice of the divine. Better yet, purchase a few and take them to your favorite shop or a homeless shelter, maybe even your local SPCA. What a surprise that would be for the recipients! And, if you get together a group of people to help you do this RAK (random act of kindness) be sure to let the media know. They'll absolutely love this 'feel-good' story.

May 25 Towel Day — Oh what a versatile item the lowly towel is. To celebrate its many uses, besides what it was intended for, have a bit of fun on your social media sites posting pics or posts of its use. If you need a list to get you started, you'll find one in Appendix A, along with a graphic you can use and share. But, above all else, wear your towel proudly today.

JUNE

Jun 27 – Jul 19 Tour de France

State Fairs

Jun 4 – 7 Nevada

Month-Long Holidays

Adopt-A-Shelter-Cat Month, *African American Music Appreciation Month, Alzheimer's and Brain Awareness Month, Audiobook Appreciation Month, Canada: National Indigenous History Month, Cancer From the Sun Month, *Caribbean American Heritage Month, Cataract Awareness Month, Child Vision Awareness Month, Dementia Care Professionals Month, Effective Communications Month, Entrepreneurs "Do It Yourself" Marketing Month, Gay and Lesbian Pride Month, *Great Outdoors Month, International Men's Month, International Surf Music Month, June Dairy Month, Men's Health Education and Awareness Month, Migraine and Headache Awareness Month, National Aphasia Awareness Month, National Bathroom Reading Month, National Candy Month, National Caribbean American Heritage Month, National Foster a Pet Month, National GLBT Book Month™, National Iced Tea Month, *National Oceans Month, National Pollinator Month, National Rivers Month, National Rose Month, National Safety Month, National Soul Food Month, National Zoo and Aquarium Month, Outdoor Marketing Month, Perennial Gardening Month, Pharmacists Declare War on Alcoholism Month, PTSD Awareness Month, Skyscraper Month, Student Safety Month

Week-Long Holidays

Jun 6 – 13 International Clothesline Week
Jun 7 – 13 Bed Bug Awareness Week, National Business Etiquette Week
Jun 13 – 20 National Hermit Week
Jun 14 – 20 Greencare for Troops Awareness Week, National Flag Week
Jun 15 – 21 Meet a Mate Week
Jun 18 – 20 Little Bighorn Days (tentative)
Jun 18 – 21 US Open
Jun 21 – 27 Craft Spirits Week
Jun 21 – 27 Lightning Safety Awareness Week (tentative)
Jun 22 – 28 National Pollinator Week, United Kingdom: National Insect Week
Jun 27 – 28 ARRL Field Day

JUNE | 29

Daily Holidays

1. Baby Boomers Recognition Day, China: International Children's Day, England: Dicing for Bibles Day, *Heimlich Maneuver Day, International Igbo Day, Kenya: Madaraka Day, Samoa: Independence Day, Say Something Nice Day, Superman Day, United Nations: Global Day of Parents, Whitmonday
2. Bhutan: Coronation Day, Germany: Waldchestag (Forest Day), Italy: Republic Day, National Gun Violence Awareness Day, Saint Erasmus Day, United Kingdom: Coronation Day, *Yell Fudge at the Cobras in North America Day (Don't laugh, I haven't seen any lately!)
3. *Chimborazo Day, Confederate Memorial Day, Global Running Day, United Nations: World Bicycle Day, Zoot Suit Riots Anniversary (1943)
4. China: Tiananmen Square Massacre (1989), Finland: Flag Day, First Free Flight by a Woman (1784), Pulitzer Prize Day (1917), Tonga: Emancipation Day, *United Nations: International Day of Innocent Children Victims of Aggression Day
5. *AIDS First Noted (1981), *Apple II (1977), Baby Boomers Recognition Day, Bahamas: Labor Day, Denmark: Constitution Day, First Balloon Flight (1783), HIV Long-term Survivors Awareness Day, National Donut Day, *United Nations: World Environment Day
6. Belmont Stakes, *Bonza Bottler Day™, *D–Day (1944), *Drive in Movie Day (1933), Korea: Memorial Day, National Trails Day, National Yo-yo Day, Prop 13 Day (1978), *SEC Day (1934), Sweden: National Day, United Nations: Russian Language Day, YMCA Day
7. Bahamas: Labor Day, *(Daniel) Boone Day, Japan: Day of the Rice God, Mackintosh Day, Malta: National Day, National Cancer Survivors Day, Orthodox Pentecost, Supreme Court Strikes Down Connecticut Law Banning Contraception (1965), Trinity Sunday
8. American Heroine Woman Rewarded (1697), Queen's Official Birthday (Selected Nations), *United Nations: World Ocean Day, *Upsy Daisy Day, World Oceans Day
9. *Donald Duck Day, International Archives Day, Pentecost, Jordan: Accession Day, National Call Your Doctor Day
10. *AA Day (1935), American Mint Day (1652), Congo: Brazzaville (Day of National Reconciliation), Jordan: Great Arab Revolt and Army Day, National Iced Tea Day, Portugal: Day of Portugal
11. Jacques Cousteau (1910), Corpus Christi, *King Kamehameha Day (First Hawaiian King), Libya: Evacuation Day, National Cotton Candy Day
12. *Baseball's First Perfect Game (1880), First Man-Powered Flight Across English Channel (1979), Loving v. Virginia Day (1967), Orlando Nightclub Massacre (2016), Paraguay: Peace with Bolivia Day, Philippines: Independence Day, Russia: Russia Day, *"Tear Down This Wall" Day, United Nations: World Day Against Child Labor
13. Roller Coaster Day (1884), United Nations: International Albinism Awareness Day
14. Alzheimer Day, Children's Day in Massachusetts, Children's Sunday, Corpus Christi (US Observance), *Family History Day, First Nonstop Transatlantic Flight (1919), First US Breach of Promise Day, *Flag Day, Japan: Rice Planting Festival, Malawi: Freedom Day, Orthodox Festival of All Saints, Race Unity Day, UNIVAC Computer Day, US Army Day, World Blood Donor Day
15. *Magna Carta Day (1215), National Prune Day, Native American Citizenship Day, *Nature Photography Day, Quarterly Estimated Federal Income Tax Payers' Due Date (also Jan 15, Apr 15, and Sep 15, 2020), United Nations: World Elder Abuse Awareness Day, US Virgin Islands: Organic Act Day
16. *Bloomsday, House Divided Speech (1858), *Ladies' Day (Baseball), South Africa: Youth Day

17. *Apartheid Day, Bunker Hill Day, Iceland: Independence Day, *United Nations: World Day to Combat Desertification and Drought
18. Battle of Waterloo Day, Egypt: Evacuation Day, Recess at Work Day, Seychelles: Constitution Day, United Nations: Sustainable Gastronomy Day
19. Belmont Stakes Day, Lou Gehrig Day, *Juneteenth, Texas: Emancipation Day, United Nations: International Day for the Elimination of Sexual Violence in Conflict, Uruguay: Artigas Day, "War is Hell" Day (1879), *World Sauntering Day
20. Argentina: Flag Day, *First Doctor of Science Earned by a Woman Day (1895), Longest Dam Race Day, *United Nations: World Refugee Day, World Juggling Day
21. Anne and Samantha Day (also Dec 21), Canada: National Indigenous Peoples Day, Father's Day, Go Skateboarding Day, Greenland: National Holiday, Midsummer Day/Eve, United Nations: International Day of Yoga, World Music Day/Fête de la Musique
22. Canada: Discover Day (Newfoundland and Labrador), Croatia: Antifascist Struggle Day, Malta: Mnarja, Stupid Guy Thing Day, US Department of Justice (150th Anniversary, 1870)
23. Estonia: Victory Day, *Let It Go Day, Luxembourg: National Holiday, National Columnists' Day, Runner's Selfie Day, United Nations: International Widows Day, United Nations: Public Service Day
24. Canada: Saint John the Baptiste Day, *Celebration of the Senses Day, China: Macau Day, "Flying Saucer" Day, Latvia: John's Day, National Energy Shopping Day, Peru: Countryman's Day, Saint John the Baptist Day, Venezuela: Battle of Carabobo Day
25. Bhutan: National Day, Korea: Tano Day, Mozambique: Independence Day, National Handshake Day, Slovenia: National Day, Supreme Court Ruling Day (Bans School Prayer, Upholds Rights to Die), Two Yugoslav Republics Declare Independence (1991), United Nations: Day of the Seafarer
26. *Barcode Day, CN Tower Day (1976), Federal Credit Union Act (1934), Human Genome Mapped (2000), Madagascar: Independence Day, National Eat at a Food Truck Day, Saint Lawrence Seaway Dedication (1959), Supreme Court Strikes Down Defense of Marriage Act (2013), Take Your Dog to Work Day®, United Nations Charter Signing (1945), *United Nations: International Day Against Drug Abuse and Illicit Trafficking, *United Nations: International Day in Support of Victims of Torture
27. *Decide to be Married Day, Djibouti: Independence Day, Great American Backyard Campout Day, *Happy Birthday to "Happy Birthday to You" Day, Industrial Workers of the World Day, *National HIV Testing Day, PTSD Awareness Day, United Nations: Micro-, Small-, and Medium-Sized Enterprises Day
28. Log Cabin Day, Monday Holiday Law (1968), Treaty of Versailles (1919)
29. *Death Penalty Ban Day, Interstate Highway System Born (1956), Saint Peter and Paul Day, Saint Peter's Day, Seychelles: Independence Day, United Nations: International Day of the Tropics
30. Asteroid Day, Britain Cedes Claim to Hong Kong (1997), Charles Blondin's Conquest of Niagara Falls (1859), Congo: Independence Day, Gone with the Wind Published (1936), Guatemala: Armed Forces Day, *Leap Second Adjustment Time Day, *NOW (National Organization of Women) Founded (1966), Sudan: Revolution Day

Holiday Marketing Ideas

National Pollinator Month—Since pollination is about helping others bloom and grow, this month focus your marketing efforts doing just that. It's time for an event that will teach your attendees how to accomplish something that has been hampering their growth. Gather together a group of diverse professionals and host an event or two. We have a full month to do get it done. So, don't let lack of time stop you.

 If you prefer you can always share tips on your social media sites. Graphics that are branded to your business always are a good idea too.

If you want to focus on the little honey making instead of money-making sort, why not provide a brochure or flyer promoting the wonders of the earth's pollinators? There are quite a few available at the pollinator.org website. I've shared the link directly to their brochures in Appendix D.

How many pollinator types can you name? There's a game in that, I think.

Jun 1 Say Something Nice Day — Our mothers always told us if you couldn't say something nice, don't say anything at all. Well, today our mothers must be gloating. This is a day to say thank you to those who make our lives better just by being a part of them, to recognize those who contribute to our lives in specific ways, and to apologize for words spoken in frustration, anger, or disappointment. Try hosting a sweet "Tweet2Win" contest, where your tweeting public can win just for saying something nice about your business. That's about the easiest thing I can think of that you can do today.

Jun 8 Upsy Daisy Day — Helping others with a leg up is a fitting way to celebrate this Weird & Wacky holiday. Uplifting messages sent to your best customers letting them know how much you appreciate them would be fitting. Send your message in a card via snail mail and it will have even more impact.

Other ways to celebrate are with seminars or webinars. Coaches and trainers alike could host an event that would showcase their businesses while giving tips and tidbits on how to do what they do. Perhaps you are an author who has written a journal. That would be a wonderful tool to share today.

Use #UpsyDaisyDay to post on social media and at the very least, SMILE! it is the easiest way I know of uplifting those around you who you share it with. You'll find a very nice graphic in Appendix A that you can use to share.

Jun 12 "Tear Down This Wall" Day — Do you have things that are stumbling blocks in your path to success? Most of us do. So, this Weird & Wacky holiday is one most business owners will find they can build a marketing plan around. Think about how you can help others to break down the wall that hampers them from achieving their full potential. If you don't personally have a product or service you can promote, I am sure you have colleagues who would be happy to address your audience.

Whether you are an artist or a business owner there is always someone who wishes they had the talent or ability you do. Why not become a mentor for them? This in turn will give you the notoriety that can set your business apart from the rest. And we all know what that can do for your bottom line.

If you've never been a mentor and would like to become one you'll find the instructions on how to do that too, in a past edition of this series. You'll find it in the 2013 edition, which is available at http://www.HolidayMarketingGuide.com, if you don't already own it.

Jun 26 Take Your Dog to Work Day®— Break out the wallet and pass your photos around! If you own a pet, just like Moms and Dads everywhere, I would bet you have at least one photo handy that you can share. Post the little lovely on your social media sites and share the love for your canine family member today. To promote your business, consider a contest for canines. There's a TV show about the most awesome dogs, so I know there's a bunch of folks out there who would love to participate and show off their beloved pet. You could do best dog trick, cutest, ugliest, or even a story about a hero dog. All these would be well received, and if you are the host, you know your business will be promoted along the way as others share your contest with their friends. You know, they are sure to say, "You've got to check this out . . . and be sure to vote for me!" So, even if they don't have a doggie friend, they're still going to see your business logo and website if you include it on all your marketing materials—which you should always do!

Jun 30 Asteroid Day— #asteroidday is the tweet of the day. Asteroid Day calls for a hundred-fold increase in asteroid monitoring.

You could give away a do-it-yourself asteroid craft that, of course, is branded to your business on your website. Then on social media tell everyone to go to your website to download it. That's one sure way to increase the traffic to your website, which is great for SEO! I have placed the template in Appendix A to make it easy for you. If you want the full-sized template email Ginger at ginger.marks@DocUmeantDesigns.com.

JULY

Jul 3 – Aug 11 Dog Days
Jul 3 – Aug 15 Air Conditioning Appreciation Days
Jul 24 – 26 Annie Oakley Days, Arcadia Daze, MI
Jul 26 – Aug 11 Pan American Games/Parapan AM Games

State Fairs

Jul 10 – 26 California
Jul 17 – 25 North Dakota
Jul 23 – Aug 1 Bangor, ME, Delaware
Jul 25 – 26 Geneva, Illinois
Jul 29 – Aug 9 Ohio
Jul 31 – Aug 8 Montana
Jul 31 – Aug 9 New Jersey

Month-Long Holidays

Alopecia Month for Women, International, Bioterrorism/Disaster Education and Awareness Month, Cell Phone Courtesy Month, Herbal/Prescription Interaction Awareness Month, National Deli Salad Month, National "Doghouse Repairs" Month, National Grilling Month, National Horseradish Month, National Hot Dog Month, National Ice Cream Month, National Make a Difference to Children Month, National Minority Mental Health Awareness Month, National Park and Recreation Month, National Watermelon Month, Smart Irrigation Month, Women's Motorcycle Month, Worldwide Bereaved Parents Awareness Month

Week-Long Holidays

Jul 5 – 11 Be Nice to Jersey Week
Jul 5 – 12 Nude Recreation Week
Jul 12 – 18 National Farrier's Week, Sports Cliché Week
Jul 18 – 25 Restless Leg Syndrome (RLS) Education and Awareness Week
Jul 18 – 26 National Moth Week
Jul 19 – 25 Captive Nations Week, Women in Baseball Week
Jul 21 – 26 Sloppy Joe's Hemmingway® Look-alike Contest
Jul 23 – 25 Japan: Soma No Umaoi (Wild Horse Chasing)
Jul 23 – 26 Comic-Con International
Jul 31 – Aug 1 Moby Dick Marathon

Daily Holidays

1. Botswana: Sir Seretse Khama Day, Burundi: Independence Day, Canada: Canada Day, Caribbean Day or Caricom Day, China: Half-year Day, *First Photographs Used in Newspaper Report (1848), *First Scheduled Television Broadcast (1941), Ghana: Republic Day, Halfway Point Day, *IRS Day (1862), Medicare Day, Postage Stamp Day, Resolution Renewal Day, Rwanda: Independence Day, Somalia Democratic Republic: National Day, Suriname: Liberation Day, *Zip Code Day, Zoo Day
2. Amelia Earhart Disappears (1937), *Civil Rights Day, *Constitution Day (USA), Declaration of Independence Resolution (1776), First Solo Round-the-World Balloon Flight (2002)
3. Air-conditioning Appreciation Days, Belarus: Independence Day, *Canada: Quebec Founded (1608), *Compliment Your Mirror Day, *Stay Out of the Sun Day
4. *America the Beautiful Day, *Anne Landers (1918), Declaration of Independence Signing (1776), Earth at Aphelion Day, *Fourth of July or Independence Day, *Independence from Meat Day, *Lou Gehrig Day (1939), Philippines: Fil American Friendship Day, United Nations: International Day of Cooperative
5. Algeria: Independence Day, *Bikini Day, Cape Verde: National Day, Ducktona 50, *National Labor Relations Day, Slovakia: Saint Cyril and Methodius Day, Venezuela: Independence Day
6. Caribbean Day or Caricom Day, Comoros: Independence Day, Czech Republic: Commemoration Day of Burning of John Hus, First Airship Crossing of the Atlantic (1919), First Successful Antirabies Inoculation (1885), Isle of Man: Tynwald Day, Lithuania: Day of Statehood, Luxembourg: Ettelbruck Remembrance Day, Malawi: Republic Day, Republican Party Day, *Take Your Webmaster to Lunch Day, Zambia: Heroes Day
7. *Bonza Bottler Day™, *Father–Daughter Take a Walk Together Day, Japan: Tanabata (Star Festival), Solomon Islands: Independence Day, Spain: Running of the Bulls, Tanzania: Saba Saba Day, Zambia: Unity Day
8. Aspinwall Crosses US on Horseback (1911), *SCUD Day (Savor the Comic, Unplug the Drama)
9. Argentina: Independence Day, First Open-Heart Surgery Day (1893), Martyrdom of the Bab, Morocco: Youth Day, South Sudan: Independence Day
10. Bahamas: Independence Day, *Clerihew Day, *Don't Step On a Bee Day, National Motorcycle Day
11. Bald is In Day, Bowdler's Day, Carver Day, *Day of the Five Billion, Make Your Own Sundae Day, Mongolia: Naadam National Holiday, Napalm Day, *United Nations: World Population Day
12. Different Colored Eyes Day, Family Feud Day (1976), Kiribati: Independence Day, Night of Nights
13. *Embrace Your Geekness Day, France: Night Watch (La Retraite Aux Flambeaux, *Gruntled Workers Day, International Town Criers Day, "Live Aid" Day, National Beef Tallow Day, National Nitrogen Ice Cream Day, Northern Ireland: Orangemen's Day, Republic of Montenegro: National Day, World Cup Day (1930)
14. England: Birmingham Riots Day (1791), France: Night Watch (Bastille Day)
15. Japan: Bon Odori (Feast of Lanterns), *Rembrandt Day, Saint Swithin's Day, Take Your Poet to Work Day, United Nations: World Youth Skills Day
16. Amazon Incorporated (1995), Atomic Bomb Test Day (75th Anniversary, 1945), Boliva: La Paz Day

17. Astor Day, Disneyland Opened (1955), Get to Know Your Customers Day (third Thursday of each quarter is set aside to get to know your customers even better), Korea: Constitution Day, Minimum Legal Drinking Age at 21 Day, Puerto Rico: Muñoz–Rivera Day, World Emoji Day, "Wrong Way" Corrigan Day (1938)
18. Mandela Day, National Bridal Sale Day, National Woodie Wagon Day, Red Skelton Day (1913), Toss Away the "Could Haves" and "Should Haves" Day, United Nations: Nelson Mandela International Day, Uruguay: Constitution Day, Women's Dive Day
19. *Art Linkletter (1912), Elvis Presley First Single Day, Italy: Feast of the Redeemer, National Ice Cream Day, Nicaragua: National Liberation Day, Saint Vincent de Paul Day
20. Columbia: Independence Day, Genva Accords (1954), Riot Act Day, *Special Olympics Day
21. Belgium: Independence Day, Guam: Liberation Day, *Hemingway Day (1899), Lowest Recorded Temperature Day (1983), No Pet Store Puppies Day
22. John Dillinger Day, *Pied Piper Day, *Rat–catchers Day, *Spooner's (Spoonerism) Day
23. Egypt: Revolution Day, *Hot Enough for Ya Day, Japan: Marine Day
24. Amelia Earhart Day, *Cousins Day, Japan: Sports Day, *National Drive-Thru Day, Pioneer Day
25. Costa Rica: Guanacast Day, First Airplane Crossing of English Channel (1909), National Day of the Cowboy, Puerto Rico: Constitution Day, Spain: Saint James Day, Tunisia: Republic Day
26. Americans with Disabilities Day, Armed Forces Unified (1947), Auntie's Day, Cuba: National Day (1953), Curaçao Day, *George Bernard Shaw (1856), Liberia and Maldives: Independence Day, Potsdam Declaration (1945), *US Army Desegregation Day (1944)
27. *Atlantic Telegraph Day, *Insulin Isolated Day (1921), *National Korean War Veterans Armistice Day, *Take Your Houseplant for a Walk Day, *Walk on Stilts Day
28. Beatrix Potter Day, Peru: Independence Day, Thailand: King's Birthday and National Day, World Hepatitis Day, World War I Begins (1914)
29. Global Tiger Day, Lord of the Rings Day, *NASA (1958), Rain Day, Spain: Festival of Near Death Experiences
30. Elvis Presley's First Concert (1954), *Emily Brontë (1818), Henry Ford Day, National Cheesecake Day, *Paperback Books (1935), Tisha B'Av, United Nations: International Day of Friendship, United Nations: World Day Against Trafficking in Persons, Vanuatu: Independence Day
31. Eid-Al-Adha, National Mutt Day, *US Patent Office Opened (1790)

Holiday Marketing Ideas

National "Doghouse Repairs" Month — Are you in the "doghouse" because you didn't do the chore you were asked to do? Well, this is the month to "get 'er done!"

In business, we also have "doghouse repairs" we should be doing for our businesses. Things like, getting rid of the clients that are more of a drain than a benefit, time management, and archiving your files, and backing up the keepers. All these and more are things we should all be doing.

So, share tips and tweets on how to do these things and more. Better yet, host a webinar or seminar jointly with other professionals to help others do these things for their own business. I bet they would appreciate learning how to fire a client, or just a reminder to back up their files. All these can be done online or off in tweets or a more in-depth event. The choice is yours.

Jul 12 – 18 Sports Cliché Week — Just for fun, keep your eye on the ball and knock it out of the park as you add as many sports clichés to your conversation as you can. Just do it just for Gipper!

I found a list of them on Wikipedia that I have placed in Appendix A to make it easy peasy for you to score a home run.

But, don't let your business become a sports cliché. Take advantage of this Weird & Wacky holiday to market your business. I have designed a full week's worth of buttons you can use to promote your business. All you have to do is add your business logo and contact information. If you want them branded in your business colors as well, give me a shout-out and I'll be happy to assist you.

Jul 3 Compliment Your Mirror Day — As we scurry through our busy schedules we often forget to take time for ourselves. Today take that time. Think about what you like about your body, not what you don't. Wear your favorite color outfit, and be sure to put on makeup if you haven't for a while. Pamper yourself with a facial or pedicure. Spend the day thinking positive thoughts about yourself. While you are at it, why not share those types of thoughts with those around you about them. Lift their spirits, make their day.

If you are a colorist, make-up seller, fashion coordinator, or even a hairstylist, this day is perfect for you. Have a training event or share tips and tweets online. Here's to focusing on the positive, your very best talents and qualities.

Jul 6 Take Your Webmaster to Lunch Day — Do you have an online business? If you don't you are definitely missing a huge marketing opportunity.

However, most of us do indeed have a go-to person that handles our online presence. Well, today is your chance to let them know how much they are appreciated. If you can't take them to lunch in person, why not send them a card with a gift certificate in it? You might somehow find out what their favorite eatery is, if you can. Otherwise, a chain restaurant is the safest bet. There's always a Starbucks close at hand, and we all know that techies live on caffeine. Do you realize that keeping your webmaster happy will do wonders for your business growth? If you can take them to lunch they might just surprise you with an idea you need to implement that will enhance your online presence. Or simply ask them how you can improve your online footprint.

Jul 17 World Emoji Day — We use emojis every day, so why not celebrate them? Join in the celebration on Twitter, Instagram or Facebook using the hashtag #WorldEmojiDay.

Try your hand at creating your own emoji or host an emoji contest. The results may surprise and amaze you. Another way to celebrate is to write a note using as many existing emojis that you can appropriately fit in. It doesn't have to be an elaborate message. It could be as simple as a button or graphic that wishes them a Happy World Emoji Day with your business logo on it.

Jul 29 Global Tiger Day— Use the hashtag #GlobalTigerDay for starters. Then to expound on that let's think about the traits of a tiger and try to come up with a way to incorporate that into our business marketing efforts. I think by now — this being the twelfth edition of the *Weird & Wacky Holiday Marketing Guide* — you have the idea of how our thought process have to work when it comes to marketing our businesses.

My go-to source for this type of information is the Chinese calendar. Hey, whatever works, eh? So, this is what I found. Tigers are powerful, tough, dynamic, mighty, determined, confident, trustworthy, frank, and sentimental; and that's the good traits. Now for the not so good we have talkative, stubborn, aggressive, and self-egotistical. So, any number of these would be options for putting together a team of speakers for a training session.

If you aren't into events, which you really should be as everyone knows how much they elevate your business and professionalism among your peers, then you could always spend the day tweeting tips or sharing graphics that are appropriate to the topic at hand. Of course, there's always sending out a card — yes, a real one — to your most valued clients and customers wishing them a Happy Global Tiger Day.

AUGUST

Aug 1 – 8 Wales: National Eisteddfod of Wales
Aug 7 – 31 Scotland: Edinburgh International Festival
Aug 13 – 30 Finland: Helsinki Festival (tentative)
Aug 29 – Oct 25 Maryland Renaissance Festival
Aug 23 – Sep 5 Luxembourg: Schuebermess Shepherd's Fair
Aug 25 – Sep 6 Paralympic Games
Aug 31 – Sep 13 US Open Tennis Championship

State Fairs

Aug –16 Wisconsin
Aug 7 – 23 Indiana
Aug 11 – 16 Vermont
Aug 11 – 15 Wyoming (& Rodeo, tentative)
Aug 13 – 23 Illinois, Iowa, Missouri
Aug 13 – 22 West Virginia (tentative)
Aug 20 – 30 Kentucky (with World's Championship Horse Show)
Aug 21 – 30 Western Idaho
Aug 22 – Oct 4 Minnesota Renaissance Festival
Aug 27 – Sep 7 Alaska, Maryland, Minnesota, Oregon
Aug 28 – Sep 7 Colorado, Nebraska, New York

Month-Long Holidays

American Adventures Month, Black Business Month, Boomers Making a Difference Month, Children's Eye Health and Safety Month, Children's Vision and Learning Month, Happiness Happens Month, International Pirate Month, National Immunization Awareness Month, National Spinal Muscular Atrophy Awareness Month, Read-A-Romance Month, What Will Be Your Legacy Month

Week-Long Holidays

Aug 1 – 7 International Clown Week (first full week), National Minority Donor Awareness Week, World Breastfeeding Week
Aug 2 – 8 National Exercise with Your Child Week
Aug 3 – 4 Antigua and Barbbuda: August Monday
Aug 3 – 9 National Bargain Hunting Week
Aug 3 – 7 Psychic Week
Aug 3 – 8 Old Fiddlers' Convention
Aug 4 – 8 World's Fair of Money

Aug 6 – 9 National Hobo Days
Aug 1 – 9 International Congress of Mathematicians 2018
Aug 2 – 4 Canada: Agrifair, National Czech Festival
Aug 2 – 10 Wales: National Eisteddfod of Wales
Aug 2 – 11 New Jersey State Fair/Sussex County Farm and Horse Show
Aug 8 – 15 England: Cowes Week
Aug 8 – 16 Elvis Week
Aug 9 – 15 Assistance Dog Week
Aug 9 – 13 Perseid Meteor Showers
Aug 15 – 21 National Aviation Week
Aug 25 – 31 Be Kind to Humankind Week
Aug 27 – 30 Hotter 'n Hell Hundred Bike Race

Daily Holidays

1. Benin: Independence Day, Emancipation of 500 Day, Fancy Farm Picnic Day, *Girlfriend's Day, *Lughnasadh, National Mustard Day, *Respect for Parents Day, Rounds Resounding Day, *Spiderman Day, Switzerland: Confederation Day, Trinidad and Tobago: Emancipation Day, United Kingdom: Minden Day, *US Census Day (1790), *US Customs Day, Word Lung Cancer Day, *World Wide Web or Internaut Day (3rd Anniversary, 2017)
2. American Family Day in Arizona, Costa Rica: Feast of Our Lady of Angels, *Declaration of Independence: Official Signing (1776), England: International Social Media Holiday, Macedonia: National Day, Saint Elias Day, Sisters' Day
3. Bahamas: Emancipation Day, Canada: Civic Holiday, Columbus Sails for the New World (1492), Colorado Day, Equatorial Guinea: Armed Forces Day, Guinea-Bissau: Colonization Martyrs' Day, Iceland and Ireland: August Holiday, Jamaica and Niger: Independence Day, National Watermelon Day, Niger: Independence Day, Zambia: Youth Day
4. Burkina Faso: Revolution Day, *Coast Guard Day, * Louis Armstrong Day, National Night Out Day, Queen Elizabeth Day
5. Burkina Faso: Republic Day, Croatia: Homeland Thanksgiving Day, First English Colony in North America (1583)
6. Atomic Bomb Day (1945), Bolivia: Independence Day, Death Penalty Day, *Hiroshima Day, *Jamaica: Independence Achieved (1962), Voting Rights Day (1965)
7. Braham Pie Day, Columbia: Battle of Boyaca Day, Cote D'Ivoire: National Day, Hatfield-McCoy Feud Eruption Day, *Mata Hari Day (1876), National Lighthouse Day, *Particularly Preposterous Packaging Day, *Professional Speakers Day, US War Department Day, World Trade Center Tightrope Walk Day
8. *Bonza Bottler Day™, Middle Children's Day, National Fried Chicken and Waffles Day, National Garage Sale Day, *Odie Day (1978), *Sneak Some Zucchini onto Your Neighbor's Porch Night, Tanzania: Farmers' Day
9. Herbert Hoover Day (Sunday nearest Aug 10th), Japan: Moment of Silence (Bombing of Nagasaki), *Moment of Silence Day, Singapore: National Day, South Africa: National Women's Day, *United Nations: International Day of The World's Indigenous People, *Veep Day
10. Bahamas: Fox Hill Day (second Tuesday in August), *Candid Camera Day, Ecuador Independence Day, Japan: Yama No Hi (Mountain Day), National S'mores Day, Nestlé Day (1814), *Smithsonian Day, Victory Day, World Lion Day

11. *Alex Haley Day (1921), Chadd: Independence Day, India: Krishna Janmashtiami, President's Joke Day, Saint Clare of Assisi: Feast Day
12. *Home Sewing Machine Day, *IBM PC Day, Night of the Murdered Poets, Thailand: Birthday of the Queen, *United Nations: International Youth Day, *Vinyl Record Day
13. *Alfred Hitchcock (1899), *Annie Oakley Day (1860), Berlin Wall Erected (1961), Central African Republic: Independence Day, *International Left Hander's Day, Lucy Stone Day (1818), Tunisia: Women's Day
14. *Navajo Nation: Code Talkers Day, Pakistan: Independence Day, *Social Security Day, V–J Day (1945)
15. *Assumption of the Virgin Mary, *Best Friends Day, *Chauvin Day, Check the Chip Day, Congo (Brazzaville): National Day, Equatorial Guinea: Constitution Day, Hirohito's Radio Address (1945), India and Korea: Independence Day, International Geocaching Day, International Homeless Animals Day® and Candlelight Vigils, Liechtenstein: National Day, *National Relaxation Day, *Panama Canal Day (1914), Transcontinental US Railway Completion (1870), *Woodstock (1969)
16. Dominican Republic: Restoration of the Republic, Klondike Gold Discovery Day, National Roller Coaster Day, Surveillance Day
17. Balloon Crossing of Atlantic Ocean (1978), Canada: Yukon Discovery Day, *Clinton's "Meaning of 'Is' Is" Day (1998), *Davy Crockett (1786), Gabon and Indonesia: Independence Day, *Mae West Day (1893)
18. *Bad Poetry Day, *Birth Control Pills Day, *Mail-Order Catalog Day, National Badge Ribbon Day, Serendipity Day
19. Afghanistan: Independence Day, *Black Cow (Root Beer Float) Day, Don Ho Day (1930), United Nations: World Humanitarian Day
20. Hungary: Saint Stephen's Day, Islamic New Year, Morocco: Revolution of the King and he People, *Plutonium Day
21. Alexandria Library Sit-in Day, *American Bar Association Day, Hawaii Admission Day Holiday, *Poet's Day, Seminole Tribe Day (1953), United Nations: International Day of Remembrance and Tribute to the Victims of Terrorism
22. *Be an Angel Day, *International Yacht Race Day, Mormon Choir Day, National Bring Your Cat to the Vet Day, *Southern Hemisphere Hoodie-Hoo Day, Vietnam Conflict Begins (1945)
23. First Man-Powered Flight (1977), Gene Kelly (1912), *United Nations: Day for the Remembrance of the Slave Trade and Its Abolition, *Valentino Day
24. Liberia: Flag Day, *Pluto Demoted Day, Ukraine: Independence Day, *Vesuvius Day, William Wilberforce Day
25. China: Double Seven Festival Day, Founders Day, *Kiss-and-Make-Up Day, *National Park Service Day, Uruguay: Independence Day, *Wizard of Oz Day (1939)
26. Baseball Day (First Televised, 1939), Nambia and Philippines: Heroes' Day, *National Dog Day, Spain: La Tomatina (Tomato Food Fight Festival) *Women's Equality Day
27. Moldova: Independence Day, *Mother Teresa Day, *"The Duchess" Who Wasn't Day
28. *March on Washington (1963), National Weed Out Hate Day, *Race Your Mouse Around the Icons Day, *Radio Commercials Day
29. *According to Hoyle Day, Ashura: Tenth Day, International Bat Night, *More Herbs, Less Salt Day, Slovakia: National Uprising Day, United Nations: International Day Against Nuclear Tests

30. 2020 Burning Man Day, Family Day in Tennessee, Huey P Long Day, Peru: Saint Rose of Lima Day, Turkey: Victory Day, United Nations: International Day of Victims of Enforced Disappearances
31. Hong Kong: Liberation Day, Kazakhstan and Kyrgyzstan: Constitution Day and Independence Day, Klondike Eldorado Gold Discovery Day, *Love Litigating Lawyers Day, Malaysia: Freedom Day, Moldova: National Language Day, Philippines; National Heroes Day, Trinidad and Tobago: Independence Day

Holiday Marketing Ideas

Happiness Happens Month — Let your joy abound! Happiness happens when we least expect it and also when we strive for it. So, to make it happen for your business this month send out cards to all your customers thanking them for their loyalty. This will bring you back to the forefront of their minds and remind them of the wonderful services and products you provide. Then, even if they don't need your help, when they meet someone else who does, you and your business will already be on their mind. And guess what that mean? You might just end up with a new customer! An email will suffice, but for real results send a real card.

Aug 1 US Census Day — It's time to look at the numbers. So, today take stock in your progress towards the goals you set for your business. Are you accomplishing them, or do you need to ramp up your efforts?

To help others do the same consider hosting a seminar/webinar. Make it motivational and educational at the same time and you'll have a win/win event for all. Topics could include time management or speaking skills, organization of workspace, proper attire, color coordinators, and many more.

Aug 3 National Watermelon Day — This speaks to me of seeds of greatness. Does that give you any inspiration? To that end tips posted throughout the day or a nice graphic shared would be simple ways to celebrate the day. You'll find a graphic that you can brand and use to make the task of posting an appropriate graphic in Appendix A.

Today is also a wonderful day to mentor a child. Speaking in a classroom setting is an easy way to do that. However, each school has different rules about school visits, so be sure you find out what they are and apply early.

Another idea that would be pretty simple to implement would be a recipe swap. If you want to get creative, you might host a class that teaches how to carve a watermelon into a basket, or any other shape you wish, which can be filled with mixed fruit. You'll find some amazing ideas on Pinterest, the link for which you'll find in Appendix D.

Aug 8 National Garage Sale Day — Here's another day you can pick a charity and raise funds for them by hosting a garage sale at your home, church, or even get a group together and make a citywide garage sale. When your event is for a charity it will be more attractive to the media to cover your event. So, do yourself proud and gather a group of civic minded friends and plan well ahead of time. You'll want to check with the charitable organization of choice to make sure you follow any guidelines they might have.

Aug 12 IBM PC Day—Today is the day back in 1981 that the IBM personal computer was introduced to the world, and we haven't been the same since. So we really should recognize this holiday, and be thankful we have them so readily available. Think of all the things we can do now at the touch of a button. Make a list of everything you have to be thankful for because you have one (or two most likely). Then post your thanks on social media throughout the day and let the world know how grateful you are that you live in a world that relies on computers on a daily basis.

Aug 15 International Geocaching Day—I took a double take on this one. It looked like a misspelling but on double checking I realized it is a real thing. What they do is do an outdoor treasure-hunting game. You search for hidden containers, called geocaches, using GPS-enabled devices. This sport fosters a strong sense of community and support for the environment.

So, the perfect solution is to create a hidden objects puzzle on your website. Then give away a valuable prize for the winner. You put the names of all the contestants who register, hint-hint: contact list building, into a hat and draw the winner from those who successfully navigate the challenge. It doesn't have to be objects, it can be answers to questions. I know of authors who use this successfully on their website and you should too!

Aug 22 Be an Angel Day—Can you do it? Can you be a good little boy or girl today? I bet you can. We can all be someone else's angel by doing random acts of kindness today. When you do, hand them a card that tells them that today is Be an Angel Day that you have also branded to your business. Or give them two and tell them to pass one along today. I've created cards and placed them in Appendix A for your use.

SEPTEMBER

Sep 15 – Oct 15 National Hispanic Heritage Month
Sep 19 – Oct 4 Oktoberfest
Sept 24 – Oct 31 Co-Op Awareness Month

State Fairs

Sep 3 – 7 Michigan (tentative), South Dakota
Sep 4 – 7 Hopkinton, NH
Sep 4 – 12 Eastern Idaho
Sep 4 – 29 Washington
Sep 10 – 0 New Mexico, Utah
Sep 11 – 20 Kansas, Tennessee
Sep 12 – 19 Southeastern Missouri District
Sep 17 – 27 Oklahoma
Sep 25 – Oct 18 Texas
Sep 25 – Oct 4 Virginia

Month-Long Holidays

Atrial Fibrillation Awareness Month, Attention Deficit Hyperactivity Disorder Month, Be Kind to Editors and Writers Month, Childhood Cancer Awareness Month, Chile: National Month, Fall Hat Month, Great American Low-Cholesterol, Low-Fat Pizza Bakd, Gynecologic Cancer Awareness Month, Happy Cat Month, Hunger Action Month, International Women's Friendship Month, Library Card Sign-Up Month, Mold Awareness Month, National Be a Food Hero Month, National Cholesterol Education Month, National DNA, Genomics & Stem Cell Education and Awareness Month, National Head Lice Prevention Month, National Honey Month, National Mushroom Month, *National Preparedness Month, National Recovery Month, National Rice Month, National Service Dog Month, National Skin Care Awareness Month, One-On-One Month, Ovarian Cancer Awareness Month, September Is Healthy Aging® Month, Shameless Promotion Month, Sports Eye Safety Month, Subliminal Communications Month, Update Your Résumé Month, Whole Grains Month, World Beach Month, Worldwide Speak Out Month

Week-Long Holidays

Sep 1 – 7 Brazil: Independence Week
Sep 2 – 5 Great Fire of London (1666)
Sep 3 – 7 Benton Hill Fair, Louisiana Shrimp and Petroleum Festival and Fair, National Sweetcorn Festival, Payson Golden Onion Days
Sep 4 – 5 Wisconsin State Coe-Chip Throw
Sep 4 – 7 Hog Capital of the World Festival, Odyssey Greek Festival, CT, Woostock Fair

Sep 5 – 7 Cleveland National Air Show
Sep 6 – 12 National Waffle Week, Substitute Teacher Appreciation Week
Sep 7 – 11 National Payroll Week
Sep 8 – 12 Play Days
Sep 13 – 19 National Security Officer Appreciation Week
Sep 13 – 19 United Kingdom: Battle of Britain Week
Sep 14 – 19 National Line Dance Week
Sep 17 – 23 Constitution Week
Sep 18 – 27 The Big E
Sep 19 – 20 Trail of Courage Living-History Festival
Sep 20 – 26 Build a Better Image Week, International Go-Kart Week, International Women's Ecommerce Days, National Farm Safety and Health Week, National Singles Week, Tolkien Week, World Reflexology Week
Sep 27 – Oct 3 Banned Books Week — Celebrating the Freedom to Read

Daily Holidays

1. Chicken Boy's Birthday, *Edgar Rice Burroughs (1875) *Emma M. Nutt Day, International Toy Testing Day, Japan: Kanto Earthquake Memorial Day, Orthodox Ecclesiastical New Year, Slovakia: Constitution Day, Titanic Discovery Day, Uzbekistan: Independence Day, WWII Begins (1939)
2. Calendar Adjustment Day, China and Taiwan: Festival of Hungry Ghosts, US Treasury Department Founded Day, Vietnam: Independence Day, *V–J Day
3. Penny Press Day (1833), Benton Neighbor Day, Qatar: Independence Day, San Marino: National Day
4. Bring Your Manners to Work Day, Curaçao: Animal's Day, Electric Lights Day, *Newspaper Carrier Day, *Paul Harvey Day
5. First Continental Congress Assembly (1774), First Labor Day Observance (1882), Jesse James Day (1847), Michigan's Great Fire of 1881, United Nations: International Day of Charity
6. Baltic States: Independence Day, Bulgaria: Unification Day, Jane Addams Day, Pakistan: Defense of Pakistan Day, Swaziland: Independence Day, United Nations: Millennium Summit (20th Anniversary, 1955)
7. Brazil: Independence Day, Canada and US: Labor Day (first Monday in September),*Google Commemoration Day (1998), *Grandma Moses Day, Mouthguard Day, *Neither Snow nor Rain Day–Day, Queen Elizabeth I Birthday (1533)
8. Andorra: National Holiday, Huey P. Long Shot Day, Macedonia: Independence Day, Malta: Victory Day, Pediatric Hematology/Oncology Nurses Day, Star Trek Day, Tarzan Day, *United Nations: International Literacy Day
9. *Bonza Bottler Day™, Japan: Chrysanthemum Day, Korea, Democratic People's Republic of: National Day, Luxembourgh: Liberation Ceremony, Tajikistan: Independence Day, *Wonderful Weirdos Day
10. Belize: Saint George's Caye Day, China: Teacher's Day, Swap Ideas Day, World Suicide Prevention Day
11. *Attack on America Day, Catalonia: National Day of Catalonia, Ethiopia: New Year's Day, *Food Stamps Day, National Day of Prayer and Remembrance, National Dog Walker Appreciation Day, *Patriot Day and National Day of Service and Remembrance

12. Defenders Day, Guinea-Bissau: National Holiday, Prairie Day, United Nations: Day for South-South Cooperation, Video Games Day
13. 9 x 13 Day, Kids Take Over the Kitchen Day, *National Celiac Awareness Day, National Grandparents' Day, Roald Dahl Day, Scooby Doo Day
14. Gravitational Waves First Detected (2015), National Boss/Employee Exchange Day, Nicaragua: Battle of San Jacinto Day, *Solo Transatlantic Balloon Crossing (1984)
15. *Agatha Christie Day, Costa Rica and El Salvador: Independence Day, *First National Convention for Blacks (1830), *Greenpeace Day (1971), Guatemala and Honduras: Independence Day, IT Professionals Day, Netherlands: Prinsjesdag, Nicaragua: Independence Day, Quarterly Estimated Federal Income Tax Payers' Due Date (also Jan 15, Apr 15, and June 15, 2020), United Kingdom: Battle of Britain Day, *United Nations: International Day of Democracy, United Nations: Opening Day of General Assembly
16. *Anne Bradstreet Day, Cherokee Strip Day, General Motors Day, *Great Seal of the US (1782), Mayflower Day (400th Anniversary, 1620), Mexico: Independence Day, National School Backpack Awareness Day, Papua New Guinea: Independence Day, *United Nations: International Day for the Preservation of the Ozone Layer, World Play-Doh Day
17. Angola: Day of the National Hero, *Citizenship Day, *Constitution Day (1787), National Constitution Center Constitution Day, National Football League Formed Day (1920), National Table Shuffleboard Day, VFW Ladies Auxiliary Day
18. Chili: Independence Day, National Cheeseburger Day, National HIV/AIDS and Aging Awareness Day, National POW/MIA Recognition (the third Friday in September), National Tradesmen Day, Rosh Hashanah (beings at sundown), *US Air Force Birthday, *US Capitol Cornerstone Laid, US Takes Out its First Loan (1789), White Woman Made American Indian Chief Day
19. *"Iceman" Mummy Discovered (1991), International Coastal Cleanup, International Red Panda Day, *International Talk Like a Pirate Day, Locate and Old Friend Day, Saint Christopher (Saint Kitts) and Nevis: Independence Day
20. *Billie Jean King Wins Battle of the Sexes (1973), Financial Panic Day, Fonzie Jumps the Shark Day, *National Equal Rights Founded (1884)
21. Armenia, Belize and Malta: Independence Day, Japan: Respect for the Aged Day, National Surgical Technologists Day, *United Nations: International Day of Peace
22. American Business Woman's Day, Dear Diary Day, *Emancipation Proclamation (1862), Hobbit Day, Ice Cream Cone Day, International Day of Radiant Peace, Japan: Autumnal Equinox Day, Long Count Day (1927), Mabon (Alban Elfed), Mali: Independence Day, National Centenarian's Day, National Walk 'n' Roll Dog Day, Remote Employee Appreciation Day, US Postmaster General's Day (1789)
23. Baseball's Greatest Dispute Day, *Celebrate Bisexuality Day, Checkers Day, Innergize Day, *Lewis and Clark Expedition Returns (1806), Planet Neptune Discovery (1846), Saudi Arabia: Kingdom Unification, United Nations: International Day of Sign Languages
24. Cambodia: Constitutional Declaration Day, Daniel Boone Day, Guinea-Bissau: Independence Day, Mozambique: Armed Forces Day, *National Punctuation Day, Remember Me Thursday®, Schwenkfelder Thanksgiving, South Africa: Heritage Day, United Nations: World Maritime Day
25. Buffalo Roundup, *First American Newspaper Published (1690), *Greenwich Mean Time Begins (1676), Hug a Vegan Day, National One Hit Wonder Day, National Psychotherapy Day, Pacific Ocean Discovered (1513) Rwanda: Republic Day

26. Fall Astronomy Day, Fish Amnesty Day, *Johnny Appleseed Day, National Hunting and Fishing Day, National Public Lands Day, United Nations: International Day for the Total Elimination of Nuclear Weapons
27. *Samuel Adams (1722), *Ancestor Appreciation Day, Ethiopia: True Cross Day, Hug a Vegan Day, Gold Star Mother's and Family Day (always the last Sunday in September), International Day of the Deaf, Saint Vincent de Paul Feast Day, *World Tourism Day, Yom Kippur (begins at sundown)
28. *Cabrillo Day, Taiwan: Confucius and Teachers' Day, United Nations/UNESCO: International Day for Universal Access to Information, World Rabies Day, Yom Kippur (begins at sundown)
29. Michelangelo Antonio (1912), Michaelmas, *National Attend Your Grandchild's Birth Day, National Biscotti Day, National Coffee Day, Paragiau" Boquerón Day, Scotland Yard Day (1829), Veterans of Foreign Wars Day
30. Botswana: Independence Day, First Criminal Execution in America Day (1630), Gutenberg Bible Published (1452), International Translation Day, Saint Jerome: Feast Day

Holiday Marketing Ideas

Fall Hat Month — Don your chapeau and strut your stuff. This is the month to wear your hats in style. Two things come to mind that you can do to celebrate your business during the month of September. First is a winter wear clothing drive for the less fortunate among us, and the second is photo sharing. One takes a bit more work than the other, but both will work equally well.

You could even do a hats for preemies craft month, if you and your friends are the crafty sort. Be sure to check with the hospital of choice for to be sure you know their requirements.

To make the photo sharing work for your business marketing efforts, turn it into a party. During the month pick one day to host a party, either online or live, where participants are requested to wear their favorite topper. The winners with the most unique, ugliest, beautiful, etc. win a prize. You could even have a contest run the entire month and give a special prize for the overall favorite. If you open the voting up to your visitors, you won't even have to judge them yourself. I have designed an image to help you promote your event which you will find in Appendix A. There's one for each type of event, the clothing drive and the hat party. I have also included a social media graphic for those of you who prefer just to share a simple graphic celebrating the month.

Sep 7 Mouthguard Day — What a great opportunity for speaking and writing coaches. Business owners who want to know how to communicate more effectively with their clients and customers will do well to attend events around this theme. And you could be on the top of their list when you host your own Mouthguard Day event.

If you want to merely do social media posts, why not share a list of the most often misused or misspelled words. That could be quite helpful. You can bet, they'll keep it. And, if you have branded your list, then guess who's name they'll have in front of them every time they refer back to it. I have placed a short list of them in the Appendix A for your use. You'll also find a couple of links to books that can help you on this subject in Appendix D.

Sep 13 9x13 Day — Everything good comes in a 9x13-inch pan. Am I right, or what? So, cook up something yummy. A sheet cake will do just fine, or maybe some mac and cheese. How about sharing your favorite recipes or better yet, get together with a group and put together a cookbook of just 9 x 13-inch pan dishes to sell with the proceeds going to your favorite charity. You could even donate the funds to a cooking school or class. Every time you share your recipes, be sure you brand them with your company name or logo. That way you'll be promoting your business as well as sharing valuable content.

Another idea is to take that yummy dish to share with others less fortunate. Do you have a sick friend or neighbor who would appreciate the gesture? You don't have to make every Weird & Wacky holiday a marketing opportunity. Sometimes a gesture of goodwill is the thing you should be doing. However, if you can't cook for them and take it to them, why not volunteer at your local food bank? If you get a group together and share the love, the media may just want to know about your efforts. And we all know what a little media attention can do for a business.

A simple graphic can be found in Appendix A for you to brand and use to in your social media postings. If you need help changing the colors or adding your logo, company name, and website send me a quick email at ginger.marks@DocUmeantDesigns.com and I'll be happy to assist you.

Sep 18 National Tradesmen Day — Today we celebrate those hardworking men and women who continue to pound the nails and work the lines. As you honor them today think about ways you can make their lives a bit easier. It could be anything from taking them a pizza for lunch to merely giving them a hug (of course, if you aren't married to one, that might be frowned upon).

Try looking up some statistics to share on social media. Some interesting tidbits I found I put into the form of an infographic you can share. Be sure to brand it for high visibility.

Sep 19 Locate an Old Friend Day — Today is a wonderful opportunity for you to reconnect with old clients and customers. I suggest you send a card out to each one wishing them a Locate an Old Friend Day and be sure to include a personal note reminding them of a service well performed or asking about something they shared with you. This will let them know they matter to you, and also bring you back to their mind, so that when they need your services again they are reminded where to go to seek help. Realize though, that your cards should reach them on or before today, so plan accordingly.

Sep 24 Remember Me Thursday® — On the heels of Locate an Old Friend Day we have Remember Me Thursday. This one is about orphaned pets though instead of people. So, today you could volunteer at your local animal shelter or even host a charity event to raise awareness and funds for one. Use #RememberMeThursday in all your social media posts. Be sure to light your candle for all to see to help shine a light on all the orphaned pets awaiting a loving home. If you have been toying with the idea to adopt a furry friend of your own, there's no better time than now.

OCTOBER

Oct 11–24 Brazil: Cirio De Nazare
Oct 24–Nov 11 World Origami Days
Oct 18 Rabi'i: The Month of Migration (begins)

State Fairs

Oct 2–25 Arizona
Oct 7–18 Mississippi
Oct 8–18 Georgia
Oct 9–18 Alabama, Arkansas
Oct 14–25 South Carolina
Oct 15–25 North Carolina
Oct 22–Nov 8 Louisiana

Month-Long Holidays

Adopt-A-Shelter-Dog Month, American Cheese Month, Antidepressant Death Awareness Month, Breast Cancer Awareness Month, Celebrating the Bilingual Child Month, Celiac Disease Awareness Month, Contact Lens Safety Month, Domestic Violence Awareness Month, Dyslexia Awareness Month, Emotional Intelligence Awareness Month, Gay and Lesbian History Month, German American Heritage Month, Global Diversity Awareness Month, Go Hog Wild — Eat Country Ham Month, Health Literacy Month, National Audiology Awareness Month/Protect Your Hearing Month, *National Breast Cancer Awareness Month, National Bullying Prevention Awareness Month, National Chiropractic Health Month, National Crime Prevention Month, *National Cybersecurity Awareness Month, National Cybersecurity Awareness Month, National Dental Hygiene Month, National Depression Education and Awareness Month, *National Disability Employment Awareness Month, *National Domestic Violence Awareness Month, National Down Syndrome Awareness Month, National Liver Awareness Month, National Medical Librarians Month, National Physical Therapy Month, National Polish American Heritage Month, National Popcorn Poppin' Month, National Reading Group Month, National Roller Skating Month, National Seafood Month, National Spina Bifida Awareness Month, National Stamp Collecting Month, National Stop Bullying Month, National Work and Family Month, Organize Your Medical Information Month, Positive Attitude Month, Rett Syndrome Awareness Month, Squirrel Awareness and Appreciation Month, Teen Services Month, Vegetarian Awareness Month, Workplace Politics Awareness Month, World Menopause Month

Week-Long Holidays

Oct 4 – 10 Fire Prevention Week, Getting the World to Beat a Path to Your Door Week, Mental Illness Awareness Week, National Carry a Tune Week, National Metric Week, United Nations: World Space Week
Oct 9 – 11 Apple Butter Makin' Days
Oct 9 – 17 Canada: Kitchener-Waterloo Oktoberfest
Oct 10 – 12 Chowder Days
Oct 10 – 17 Take Your Medicine Americans Week
Oct 11 – 17 Earth Science Week, Emergency Nurses Week, National Food Bank Week
Oct 12 – 16 National School Lunch Week
Oct 14 – 18 Germany: Frankfurt Book Fair
Oct 15 – 20 Japan: Newspaper Week
Oct 17 – 24 Food and Drug Interaction Education and Awareness Week
Oct 18 – 24 Bullying Bystanders Unite Week, National Character Counts Week, National Chemistry Week, National Forest Products Week, Rodent Awareness Week
Oct 19 – 23 Nuclear Science Week
Oct 24 – 31 Prescription Errors Education and Awareness Week
Oct 24 – 30 United Nations: Disarmament Week
Oct 25 – 31 International Magic Week

Daily Holidays

1. China, People's Republic of: National Day, Cyberspace Day, Cyprus: Independence Day, *Fire Pup Day, Korea: Chusok, Model-T Day, Nigeria: Independence Day, Night of the Living Dead Day, South Korea: Armed Forces Day, This is Your Life Day, Tuvalu: Independence Day, United Kingdom: National Poetry Day & International Day of Older Persons, US 2021 Federal Fiscal Year Begins, World Vegetarian Day
2. Gandhi Day, *Guardian Angels Day, *Groucho Marx (1890), Guinea: Independence Day, Kids Music Day, *National Custodial Workers Day, National Diversity Day, *"Peanuts" Debut Day (1950), Sukkot (begins at sundown), 'Twilight Zone' Day, United Nations: International Day of Nonviolence, World Day for Farmed Animals, World Smile Day
3. Bed & Breakfast Inn Mascot Day, Captain Kangaroo Day, Germany: Day of German Unity, Honduras: Francisco Morazán Holiday, Korea: Tangun Day (National Foundation Day), *Mickey Mouse Club Day (1955), Netherlands: Relief of Leiden Day, Sukkot (begins at sundown), Woofstock
4. Blessing of the Fishing Fleet, Country Inn, Bed-and-Breakfast Day, *Dick Tracy Day (1931), Germany: Erntedankfest, *Greorgian Calendar Adjustment Day, International Ships-In-Bottles Day, Lesotho: Independence Day, National Taco Day, Saint Francis of Assisi: Feast Day, *Ten-Four Day. World Child Development Day, World Communion Sunday
5. Blue Shirt Day™/World Day of Bullying Prevention™, Child Health Day (first Monday in October), Duputren Disease Awareness Day, James Bond Day, Portugal: Republic Day, United Nations: World Habitat Day *United Nations: World Teachers Day
6. *American Library Association Day, Egypt: Armed Forces Day, Ireland: Ivy Day, *Jackie Mayer Rehab Day, *National German American Day, National G.O.E. (Growth.Overcome.Empower.) Day, National Noodle Day, National Plus Size Appreciation Day, United Kingdom: National Badger Day

7. Croatia: Statehood Day, National Forgiveness and Happiness Day
8. Ada Lovelace Day, *Alvin C. York Day, Croatia: Statehood Day, *Great Chicago Fire (1871), National Depression Screening Day, National Hydrogen and Fuel Cell Day, National Pierogy Day, National Salmon Day, Peshtigo Forest Fire (1871)
9. *Leif Erickson Day, Korea: Hangul (Alphabet Day), National Nanotechnology Day, Peru: Day of National Honor, Uganda: Independence Day, *United Nations: World Post Day
10. *Bonza Bottler Day™, *Double 10 Day, Legends and Lanterns Day Night (also Oct 17 & 23), Motorsport Memorial Day, National Cake Decorating Day, National Handbag Day, *Tuxedo Day, *US Naval Academy Day, World Day Against the Death Penalty, *World Mental Health Day
11. *Adding Machine Day, *General Pulaski Memorial Day, Grandmother's Day in Florida, *National Coming Out Day, Samoa and American Samoa: White Sunday, Southern Food Heritage Day, United Nations: International Day of the Girl Child
12. American Indian Heritage Day (Alabama), Bahamas Discovery Day, Canada: Thanksgiving Day, Columbus Day (Observed and Traditional), *Day of the Six–Billion, Discoverer's Day in Hawaii, Equatorial Guinea: Independence Day, Fiji: Independence Day, *International Moment of Frustration Scream Day, Mexico: Dia de la Raza, National Kick Butt Day, Native Americans' Day (South Dakota), Spain: National Holiday, Virgin Islands-Puerto Rico Friendship Day, Yorktown Victory Day
13. Ada Lovelace Day, *Jesse Leroy Brown Day, International Face Your Fears Day, *Navy Birthday, United Nations: International Day for Natural Disaster Reduction, Whitehouse Cornerstone Laid (1792)
14. *Be Bald and Be Free Day, Emergency Nurses Day, National Bring Your Teddy Bear to Work Day, National Bullying Prevention Day, National Fossil Day, National Take Your Parents to Lunch Day, Sound Barrier Broken (1947), Supersonic Skydive Day (2012)
15. *Blind Americans Equality Day (formerly White Cane Safety Day), First Manned Flight (1783), Get Smart About Credit Day, Get to Know Your Customers Day (third Thursday of each quarter is set aside to get to know your customers even better), National Grouch Day, United Nations: International Day of Rural Women
16. Birth Control Day (1916), Dictionary Day, Global Cat Day, Million Man March (1995), Missouri Day, *National Boss' Day, National Mammography Day, Noah Webster Day, United Nations: World Food Day
17. 300 Millionth American Born (2006), Black Poetry Day, Evel Knievel Day, Bridge Day, Legends and Lanterns Day Night (also Oct 10 & 23), *Mulligan Day, National Playing Card Collection Day, San Francisco 1989 Earthquake (1989), Sweetest Day, *United Nations: International Day for the Eradication of Poverty
18. Azerbaijan: Independence Day, Birth of Bab, Canada: Persons Day (1929), Comic Strip Day, Saint Luke Feast Day, Water Pollution Control Day, *World Menopause Day
19. Alaska Day (observed), Evaluate Your Life Day, Jamaica: National Heroes Day, LGBT Center Awareness Day, Virgin Islands: Hurricane Thanksgiving Day, Yorktown Day
20. John Dewey Day, Guatemala: Revolution Day, Kenya: Mashujaa Day, Miss America Rose Day, United Nations: World Statistics Day
21. Hagfish Day, *Incandescent Lamp Day, Missouri Day, Taiwan: Overseas Chinese Day
22. *International Stuttering Awareness Day, Smart is Cool Day, World's End Day
23. Cambodia: Peace Treaty Day, Hungary: Republic Day (Declares Independence), *IPod Day, National Mole Day, Legends and Lanterns Day Night (also Oct 10 & 17), Swallows Depart from San Juan Capistrano, Thailand: Chulalongkorn Day

24. First Barrel Jump over Niagara Falls (1901), Recycle Your Mercury Thermostat Day, United Nations Day, *United Nations: World Development Information Day
25. China: Chung Yeung Festival (Double Nine Day), European Union: Daylight Savings Time Ends, First Female FBI Agents (1972), India: Dasara (Dussehra), Mother-in-Law Day, Picasso Day, Reformation Sunday, Saint Crispin's Day, Sourest Day, Taiwan: Retrocession Day
26. Austria: National Day, Erie Canal Day, Gunfight at the O.K. Corral (1881), Mule Day, New Zealand: Labor Day, Zambia: Independence Day
27. *Cranky Coworkers Day, *Navy Day, Saint Vincent and the Grenadines & Turkmenistan: Independence Day, United Nations: World Day for Audiovisual Heritage, *Walt Disney Day
28. Czech Republic: Independence Day, Greece: Ochi Day, *Saint Jude's Day, Statue of Liberty Dedication (1886)
29. *Internet Created (50th Anniversary, 1969), National Cat Day, Turkey: Republic Day
30. Checklists Day, *Create A Great Funeral Day, Devil's Night, *Emily Post Day, Frankenstein Friday, *Haunted Refrigerator Night, National Candy Corn Day, "War of the Worlds" (1938) World Audio Drama Day
31. *Books for Treats Day, "Car Talk" Day, *Halloween, Houdini Day, *Magic Day, Mount Rushmore Day, *National Knock–Knock Day, *Reformation Day, Samhain, Sweden: All Saints' Day, Taiwan: Chiang Kai-Shek Day, Trick or Treat or Beggar's Night, United Nations: World Cities Day

Holiday Marketing Ideas

Organize Your Medical Information Month — This is so very important to do that getting the word out about this month-long holiday is the right thing to do. I suggest you create wallet sized cards that are branded for this purpose to give out to everyone you come in contact with today. You can hand physical copies out of make them downloadable. I suggest you give out a sheet of them as typically our information changes often.

I have provided you with organizational binder tabs to make it easy to organize your medical records, which, of course, is in Appendix A. You'll also find there a wallet sized and a business card sized medical information card you can brand and disseminate.

Oct 2 World Smile Day — What a great holiday to start the fall holiday season! Flash your pearly (or not so pearly) whites all day long. Get rid of the grump and make someone's day with the best tool you have, your smile. There you have another idea, ways to get rid of the grump. You could post tips on relaxation or overcoming obstacles. Heck, why not make an event out of it? And of course, be sure to brand any graphics you share so that when they go viral so will your business contact information.

Oct 5 United Nations: World Teachers Day — Today we celebrate teachers everywhere and their contribution and dedication to education. So, today share your appreciation in whatever way you see fits your connection with the educators around you. Anything from a simple thank you card to cupcakes will do the trick. But, if you want to brand your business (or if you are an author, your

book), I suggest you greet them in person so when you approach them with your idea to share with their classes they will be open to the possibility.

Another way you could celebrate is to have your own teach-in. An event is always, always, a great idea to get your business noticed. Gather together a group of speakers on any topic you know your tribe will want to hear and promote it ahead of time. When you host or sponsor an event you will get noticed!

Oct 8 National Hydrogen and Fuel Cell Day—Where would we be without energy? Clean, renewable energy is good for the environment, which, in turn, is good for people. All this is made possible through today's technological advances. So, as you look at celebrating this Weird & Wacky holiday, consider using your physical energy to clean up the environment around you. Any environmentally friendly event, today, will get the media's attention, if you let them know. Gather a group and sponsor a beach clean-up, or speak at schools. Either could be good for your business as well as the world around you.

However, if events are not in your marketing plan social media is there to make things easy. Simply post graphics, and words of wisdom about the impact sustainable energy makes our world safer and cleaner.

Oct 12 National Kick Butt Day—This is the day to stop procrastinating and get the chore done that you have been putting on hold. Kick any negative feelings you have in the butt. And I mean kick! That makes today is a great time to either host or sponsor a seminar on time management and organizational skills. Helping others put together their business or marketing plan is another option for your must do event. Perhaps you have a novel in you that you have been meaning to write. A writing workshop would fit your need quite nicely. When you host or sponsor events like these your business will get noticed. At the very least use social media to your advantage by posting your custom graphic with your business logo on it to share. Talking about social media, don't forget to use #NationalKickButtDay when you post.

Oct 19 Evaluate Your Life Day—It's time to reevaluate your priorities, put things in order, and rethink your business plan. As you begin to think about the changes you need to make to catapult your business and life to your vision of success why not help others along the way. Consider becoming a mentor to someone who needs a leg up. If you are up to an event, perhaps scheduling a joint venture speaking engagement is perfect for you. All the topics mentioned before would make for great subjects for your event. Perhaps you are a career coach or job recruiter, host a training on resume writing or even interview training, or a exercise trainer, host a free evaluation day? There are many young people who could use the advice you could give.

One sure way to spend the day, or at least an hour of it, is to do a Personal SWOT Analysis. This will help you assess where you need improvement. You'll find this form in Appendix A courtesy of mindtools.com. Perhaps you need to work on attracting new clients. That would be a good subject for a seminar or webinar all by itself. Or what about reassessment of your time? Are you using your time wisely? Are you spending too much time on social media and not enough getting on with your business and life? These too are areas that many of us need improvement. Or what about how to automate a process you are manually doing? There are quite a few ways you can help yourself and others as you celebrate this Weird & Wacky holiday.

As you celebrate this Weird & Wacky holiday you may find that your focus needs to be more geared toward social media. If that's the case, then look for ways to offer advice or encouragement to others. And by all means, post those branded messages and graphics to keep your name out there where others can see it often. You'll find a graphic you can freely use in Appendix A.

Oct 31 "Car Talk" Day—If you've been wanting to start your own podcast today is the day to make your dream a reality. Perhaps your goal is to get onto a podcast as a guest. Today is the day to start working your way towards that end. If you are a podcast or radio host today is YOUR day! Promote the heck out of your show and watch your demographics grow.

NOVEMBER

Nov 21 – Dec 30 Germany: Duisburg Christmas Market
Nov 28 – Dec 6 Mexico: Guadalajara International Book Fair
Nov 25 – Dec 23 Germany: Frankfurt Christmas Market

Month-Long Holidays

American Diabetes Month, Aviation History Month, Banana Pudding Lovers Month, Diabetic Eye Disease Month, Eye Donation Month, Lung Cancer Awareness Month, *National Adoption Month, National Epilepsy Awareness Month, *National Family Caregivers Month, National Georgia Pecan Month, National Inspirational Role Models Month, National Long-Term Care Awareness Month, National Marrow Awareness Month, National Memoir Writing Month, *National Native American Heritage Month, National Novel Writing Month, National Runaway Prevention Month, Peanut Butter Lovers' Month, PPSI/ACA Aids Awareness Month, Prematurity Awareness Month, World Vegan Month, Worldwide Bereaved Siblings Awareness Month

Week-Long Holidays

Nov 1 – 7 Polar Bear Week
Nov 2 – 6 National Patient Accessibility Week
Nov 9 – 13 National Young Reader's Week
Nov 13 – 15 National Donor Sabbath
Nov 13 – 19 World Antibiotic Awareness Week (tentative)
Nov 16 – 20 American Education Week
Nov 22 – 28 National Family Week, National Game & Puzzle Week
Nov 23 – 28 Better Conversation Week
Nov 29 – Dec4 Netherlands: Midwinter Horn Blowing

Daily Holidays

1. Algeria: Revolution Day, *All Hallows or All Saints Day, Antigua and Barbuda: Independence Day, European Union (1993), Daylight Savings Time Ends, European Union Day, Extra Mile Day, Lisbon Earthquake (1755), Mexico: Day of the Dead, Movember, *National Authors' Day, National Forgiveness and Happiness Day, National Sports Fan Day, US Virgin Islands: Liberty Day, Zero Tasking Day
2. *All Souls Day, Australia: Recreation Day, Daniel Boone Day, *First Scheduled Radio Broadcast (1920), National Traffic Professionals Day, United Nations: International Day to End Impunity for Crimes Against Journalists

3. Canada: New Inuit Territory Approved (1992), *Cliché Day, Dewey Day, Dominica: National Day, General Election Day, *Japan: Culture Day, Micronesia and Panama: Independence Day, Public Television Day, *Sandwich Day, SOS Day
4. Italy: Victory Day, *King Tut Tomb Discovery (1922), Mischief Night, *National Chicken Lady Day, National Easy Bake Oven Day, Panama: Flag Day, Russia: Unity Day, UNESCO Day, *Will Rogers (1879)
5. El Salvador: Day of the First Shout for Independence, *England: Guy Fawkes Day, National Men Make Dinner Day, Return Day, *Roy Rogers (1911), *Shattered Backboard Day, United Nations: World Tsunami Awareness Day, Vivian Leigh–Scarlett O'Hara Day (1913)
6. Morocco: Anniversary of the Green March, National Medical Science Liaison (MSL) Awareness and Appreciation Day, Samoa: Arbor Day, Saxophone Day, Sweden: Gustavus Adolphus Day, *United Nations: International Day for Preventing the Exploitation of the Environment in War and Armed Conflict
7. Bangladesh: Solidarity Day, First Black Governor Elected (1989), Madam Curie Day, National Bison Day, Pumpkin Destruction Day, Republican Symbol (1874), Russia: Revolution Day, Sadie Hawkins Day
8. Abet and Aid Punsters Day, Cook Something Bold and Pungent Day, Shakespeare Authorship Mystery Day, *X–ray Day
9. *Berlin Wall Opened (1989), Boston Fire (1872), Cambodia: Independence Day, East Coast Blackout (1965), Germany: Kristallnacht, National Child Safety Council Day
10. *Area Code Day (1951), Claude Rains Day, Marine Corps Day, Panama: First Shout of Independence, Sesame Street Anniversary (1969), United Nations: World Science Day for Peace and Development
11. Angola: Independence Day, *Bonza Bottler Day™, Canada: Remembrance Day, China: Singles Day, Columbia: Cartagena Independence Day, Death/Duty Day, England: Remembrance Day, God Bless America Day, Japan: Origami Day, Maldives: Republic Day, Martinmas, Poland: Independence Day, Sweden: Saint Martin's Day, Switzerland: Martinmas Goose (Martinigians), Veterans Day (1919)
12. Mexico: Postman's Day, Sun Yat-Sen (traditional), World Pneumonia Day
13. Holland Tunnel Day
14. Claude Monet Day, Dow Jones Tops 1,000 (1642), Guinea-Bissau: Readjustment Movement's Day, India: Children's Day, India: Diwali (Deepavali), International Girls Day, Loosen Up Lighten Up Day, Moby Dick Day, National Block It Out Day, *United Nations: World Diabetes Day
15. *America Recycles Day, Belgium: Dynasty Day, Brazil: Republic Day, George Spelvin Day, Germany: Volkstrauertag, Japan: Shichi–Go–San (Seven-Five-Three) Day, United Nations: World Day of Remembrance for Road Traffic Victims
16. Estonia: Day of National Rebirth, Israel: Sigd, *Lewis and Clark Expedition Reaches Pacific Ocean (1805), Saint Eustatius, *United Nations: International Day for Tolerance
17. *Homemade Bread Day, National Unfriend Day, Suez Canal Day, World Prematurity Day
18. Germany: Buss Und Bettag, Haiti: Army Day, Latvia: Independence Day, *Married to a Scorpio Support Day, *Mickey Mouse's Birthday (1928), National Book Awards Announcement Day, National Educational Support Professionals Day, Oman: National Holiday, US Uniform Time Zone Plan (1883)
19. Belize: Garifuna Day, Cold War Ends (1990), *Dedication Day (1862), First Automatic Toll Collection Machine (1954), Gandhi Day, Garfield Day, Great American Smoke-out (third

Thursday), *"Have A Bad Day" Day, Monaco: National Holiday, Puerto Rico: Discovery Day, United Nations: World Toilet Day, World Philosophy Day

20. *Bill of Rights Day, Edwin Powell Hubble Day, *Mandelbrot Day (1924), Mexico: Revolution Day, *Name Your PC Day, Substitute Educators Day, Transgender Day of Remembrance, *United Nations: African Industrialization Day, United Nations: Universal Children's Day
21. Dow Jones Tops 5,000, *Sir Samuel Cunard (1787), Thailand: Elephant Roundup at Surin, *United Nations: World Television Day, World Hello Day
22. Charles De Gaulle Day 1890), Edward Teach "Blackbeard" Death, (1718), *George Eliot (1819), Humane Society of the US Day (1954), Germany: Totensonntag, Lebanon: Independence Day, Stir It Up Sunday
23. Billy the Kid Day, Fibonacci Day, Boris Karloff Day, Fibonacci Day, Harpo Marx Day, International Aura Awareness Day, Japan: Labor Thanksgiving Day, Switzerland: Zibelemarit (Onion Market)
24. *Celebrate Your Unique Talent Day, *Dale Carnegie (1888), *D.B. Cooper Day
25. *Andrew Carnegie (1835), Bosnia and Herzegovina: National Day, *JFK Day (1960), Saint Catherine's Day, Suriname: Independence Day, Tie One On Day™, United Nations: International Day for the Elimination of Violence Against Women Day
26. Charles Schultz (1922), Mongolia: Republic Day, Thanksgiving Day
27. Black Friday, Bruce Lee Day, Buy Nothing Day (27–28), Dine Over Your Kitchen Sink Day, Face Transplant Day, Family Day in Nevada, Laerdal Tunnel Opening (2000), National Flossing Day, Native American Heritage Day, Slinky™ Day
28. *Albania: Independence Day, Chad: Republic Day, International Aura Awareness Day, *Lévi-Strauss (1908), Mauritania: Independence Day, Panama: Independence from Spain, Small Business Saturday
29. Advent First Sunday, Alcott Day, *CS Lewis (1898), *Electronic Greetings Day, Handel's Messiah Sing-Along Day, *United Nations: International Day of Solidarity with the Palestinian People
30. Articles of Peace Between Great Britain and the US (1782), Barbados: Independence Day, Computer Security Day, Cyber Monday, Philippines: Bonifacio Day, Saint Andrew's Day, *Stay Home Because You're Well Day, United Nations: Day of Remembrance for all Victims of Chemical Warfare

Holiday Marketing Ideas

Eye Donation Month — Are you an organ donor? Have you signed your advanced directives? Why not make this the month to help others make this important decision? Get involved with organizations that support and help others complete the necessary paperwork. You can even take your laptop or iPad with you and have them complete the forms online. I've put the link in Appendix A. When you do this make sure the media knows you and your team are about this month. They are sure to want to highlight you in a segment.

Other ideas you might consider are seminar/webinars that focus on seeing clearly the direction they need to take to reach their lofty goals.
Some suggestions would be business or marketing planning, journaling, re-evaluating their mission statement, and scheduling.

At the very least you might share tips on eye care, especially if you have any vision related business. Glaucoma and cataracts are major concerns for the elderly. Then, there's always the tried and true infographic that you can brand to your business. I have included an excellent one I found at piedmont.org that I have placed in Appendix A.

Nov 1 National Forgiveness and Happiness Day — Unforgiveness hurts the withholder more than the person who is unforgiven. So, today is a day to set aside the animosity and move forward. Holding a grudge causes not just emotional issues, but it can also manifest in physical ailments. Stress is just one of the side effects. As you look to how to promote your business today consider meditation or stress relief training as an option. Whether you are the host, speaker, or sponsor of these types of events, or you choose to host a make-up or scented candle party these types of events can heal the body and soul.

Nov 2 National Traffic Professionals Day — Getting traffic to our websites is always a challenge. There are many resources out there to help you make that happen. But, if you and your colleagues don't know how, today is a terrific day to take the initiative and schedule an event that presents people in the know. This has got to be the best way to market your business today.

Another option is to create a search and find on your website. Simply create questions that the answers can be found on your website and invite others to participate. Then those who come up with all the correct answers, their names and emails go into a drawing for a significant award. See, you have just collected a bunch of contacts who can now be marketed to, but only if you let them know that is included in the contest (you will receive news and opportunities in the future).

What about getting a group of like-minded individuals together and put a small package of items together and hand them out to crossing guards in your area? If you do that be sure to let the media know what you are up to. They love "feel-good" stories, and this could be one of the best!

Nov 7 Sadie Hawkins Day — While Sadie Hawkins Day is about girls turning the tables on boys by asking them out, may I suggest that you step up to the task by asking for the help you deserve? It's time to stop letting things get in your way; ask for what you want and need. At the very least you'll get turned down, at the very most, you'll get what you seek.

So, as you think along those lines, think about ways you can help others do just that. Perhaps you know how to instill confidence, or you can show others how to do something that they always wanted to learn. Hosting or sponsoring events, as I have said before, is the very best way to get your business noticed. They prove your expertise and that will make you stand out from the crowd.

Social media postings and graphics are another easy way to celebrate this Weird & Wacky holiday. Just be sure to brand them to your business so when they are shared your name goes with them.

Nov 14 Loosen Up Lighten Up Day — All work and no play makes for a dull life. So today relax, let your hair down, and spend the day doing what you wish you could do all year long. As you consider that stress plays a major part of the reason this Weird & Wacky holiday was created, if you have anything to do with stress relief, exercise or business coach, public speaking trainer, candle seller, aroma therapist, massage therapist, etc., you'll find today an excellent choice to ramp up your marketing efforts.

For those of us who don't fit that ilk, social media graphics and tip sheets would be a viable alternative. To make it easier for you to share, you'll find an infographic in Appendix A that you can brand and share.

Nov 22 Stir It Up Sunday — Whilst this day is traditionally about the making of Christmas pudding on the last Sunday before Advent begins, it also is about stirring things up a bit. So, thinking along these lines, consider ways you can stir up a few new clients or customers. What immediately comes to my mind is an event that will get people motivated.

Other than a whirlwind event, you could always share motivational quotes throughout the day. That would probably be the easiest way to celebrate. If you create them as social media graphics so much the better. Just be sure to brand them with your company information so that when they are shared so is your contact information.

Nov 28 International Aura Awareness Day — When you let your light shine you light up the world around you. So, send out cards and email, letters and notes that share your good thoughts with your customers and clients. Wish them a happy International Aura Awareness Day especially if you are a healer, nutritionist, or sensitive. Coaches and trainers too would do well to focus on this Weird & Wacky holiday. Positive vibes are always welcome, and today is the perfect day to send some out to everyone you touch.

DECEMBER

Dec 1 – Jan 6 Netherlands: Midwinter Horn Blowing
Dec 14 – Jan 5, 2021 Christmas Bird Count
Dec 14 – 28 Halcyon Days
Dec 17 – Feb 2, 2020 Take a New Year's Resolution to Stop Smoking (TANYRSS)

Month-Long Holidays

Bingo's Birthday Month, *National Impaired Driving Prevention Month, National Write a Business Plan Month, Safe Toys and Gifts Month, Worldwide Food Service Safety Month, National Vinegar Month

Week-Long Holidays

Dec 3 – 10 Clerc-Gallaudet Week
Dec 7 – 11 National Older Driver Safety Awareness Week
Dec 11 – 18 Chanukah
Dec 17 – 23 Saturnalia
Dec 26 – Jan 1, 2021 Kwanzaa

Daily Holidays

1. Antarctica Day, *Basketball Day, *Bifocals at the Monitor Liberation Day, Canada: Yukon Order of Pioneers (1894), *Civil Air Patrol Day, Giving Tuesday, Portugal: Independence Day, Romania: National Holiday, Rosa Parks Day, *United Nations: World AIDS Day
2. *Artificial Heart Transplant Day (1967), Central African Republic: National Day Observed, England: Walter Plinge Day, Laos: National Day, *Joseph Bell (1837), National Mutt Day—December, *Special Education Day, United Arab Emirates: Independence Day, *United Nations: International Day for the Abolition of Slavery Day
3. Be a Blessing Day, E-Discovery Day, First Heart Transplant (1967), *United Nations: International Day of Persons with Disabilities
4. Ghana: National Farmers' Day, Mary Celeste Discovery Day, National Grange Day, National Sales Person's Day, Saint Barbara's Day, *Samuel Butler (1835)
5. *AFL–CIO Founded (1955), Austria: Krampuslauf, *Bathtub Party Day, Bike Shop Day, Haiti: Discovery Day, "Irrational Exuberance" Day, Montgomery Bus Boycott Remembrance Day, *United Nations: International Volunteer Day for Economic and Social Development, United Nations: World Soil Day, *Walt Disney (1901)
6. Christmas to Remember Day, Ecuador: Day of Quito: Founding (1534), Finland: Independence Day, Missouri Earthquakes (1811), *National Miners' Day, *National Pawnbrokers Day, *Saint Nicholas Day, Spain: Constitution Day

7. Armenian Earthquake (1988), Central African Republic: National Day (observed), Cote D'Ivoire: Commemoration Day, Iran: Students Day, *National Fire Safety Council Day (1979), *National Pearl Harbor Remembrance Day, *United Nations: International Civil Aviation Day
8. AFL Day, *Eli Whitney (1765), Feast of Immaculate Conception, Guam: Lady of Camarin Day, Intermediate-Range Nuclear Forces Treaty (INF) Signed (1987), NAFTA Day, National Lard Day, Soviet Union Dissolved (1991), Uzbekistan: Constitution Day
9. Birdseye Day, Tanzania: Independence and Republic Day, *United Nations: International Anti-Corruption Day, United Nations: International Day of Commemoration and Dignity of the victims of the Crime of Genocide and of the Prevention of this Crime
10. *Ada Lovelace (1815), Chanukah (begins at sundown), *Dewey Decimal System Day, *Emily Dickinson (1830), Encyclopedia Britannica First Published (1879), *Human Rights Day, James Addams Day, *Nobel Prize Awards Ceremonies, *Thomas Hopkins Gallaudet (1787), Thailand: Constitution Day, *United Nations: Human Rights Day
11. Burkino Faso: Independence Day, Kaleidoscope Day, Official Lost and Found Day, *UNICEF Birthday, *United Nations: International Mountain Day
12. *Bonza Bottler Day™, Day of Our Lady of Guadalupe, Gingerbread Decorating Day, Kenya: Jamhuri Day (Independence Day), Mexico: Guadalupe Day, National Day of the Horse, *Poinsettia Day, *Puerto Rico: Las Mañanitas, Turkmenistan: Neutrality Day, United Nations: International Day of Neutrality, United Nations: International Universal Health Coverage Day
13. Malta: Republic Day, *New Zealand Discovery (1642), Sweden: Saint Lucia Day
14. *Doolittle Day, Nostradamus (1503), South Pole Discovery (1911)
15. *Bill of Rights Day, *Cat Herders Day, Curaçao: Kingdom Day and Antillean Flag Day, Puerto Rico: Navidades
16. Bahrain: Independence Day, Bangladesh: Victory Day, *Barbie and Barney Backlash Day, Boston Tea Party Day, Calabria Earthquake (1857), *Jane Austen (1775), Kazakhstan: Independence Day, *Ludwig Van Beethoven (1770), Mexico: Posadas, Philippines; Philippine Christmas Observance and Simbang Gabi, South Africa: Reconciliation Day, *United Nations: Zionism Day
17. *Azteck Calendar Stone Discovery Day (1790), *Clean Air Day, First Flight Anniversary Celebration Day, *Joseph Henry (1797), Libby Day, Take a New Year's Resolution to Stop Smoking (TANYRSS) Day, *Wright Brothers Day
18. *Benjamin O Davis, Jr. (1912), *Joseph Grimaldi (1778), Mexico: Feast of Our Lady of Solitude, Niger: Republic Day, "To Tell the Truth" Day, Underdog Day, United Nations: Arabic Language Day, *United Nations: International Migrants Day
19. Titanic Day
20. American Poet Laureate Day, Montgomery Bus Boycott Ends (1956), *Mudd Day, *United Nations: International Human Solidarity Day
21. Celebrate Short Fiction Day, Benjamin Disraeli Birth (1804), *Crossword Puzzle Day, *Forefathers Day, *Heinrich Böll (1917), *Humbug Day, *Phileas Fogg Win a Wager Day, Pilgrim Landing, Shorts Day, United Kingdom Allows Same-Sex Civil Partherships Day, Yalda, Yule
22. Be a Lover of Silence Day, First Gorilla Born in Captivity (1956), *Giacomo Puccini (1858), Oglethorpe Day
23. *Federal Reserve System (1913), Festivus Day, First Non-stop Flight Around the World (1987), Metric Conversion Act (1975), Mexico: Feast of Radishes, *Transistor Day (1947)

24. Austria: "Silent Night, Holy Night", *Christmas Eve, First Surface-to-Surface Guided Missile, *James Prescott Joule (1818), Libya: Independence Day
25. *A'Phabet Day or No-L-Day, Asarah B'Tevet, *Christmas Day, Cuba: Christmas Returns, Taiwan: Constitution Day, Washington Crosses the Delaware (1776)
26. *Bahamas: Junkanoo, Boxing Day, Ireland: Day of the Wren, Luxembourg: Blessing of the Wine, National Candy Cane Day, *National Whiner's Day, Radium Discovery Day, Saint Stephen's Day, Second Day of Christmas, Slovenia: Independence Day, South Africa: Day of Goodwill, *United Kingdom: Boxing Day
27. "Howdy Doody" Day, *Johannes Kepler (1571), *Louis Pasteur (1822), Saint John Feast Day
28. Australia: Proclamation Day, *Cinema Day, Endangered Species Day, *Holy Innocents Day or Childermas, *Pledge of Allegiance Day
29. Andrew Johnson Wreath-Laying, Saint Thomas of Canterbury: Feast Day, *Tick Tock Day, *YMCA Day
30. *Falling Needles Family Fest Day, *Rudyard Kipling (1865), "Let's Make a Deal" Day, Philippines: Rizal Day, USSR DAY (1922)
31. *First Nights, First US Bank Opens (1781), *Japan: Namahage, *Leap Second Adjustment Time Day, *Make Up Your Mind Day, *New Year's Eve, New Year's Eve Banished Words List Day, No Interruptions Day, Pie Fight Day, Saint Sylvester's Day, Scotland: Hogmany

Holiday Marketing Ideas

Bingo's Birthday Month — Seniors everywhere know how much fun and excitement can be had with a simple game of Bingo. Anticipation, dedication, and cheer are all part of the game. Simply speaking, this month is the month to focus on getting the job done. A fun thing to do would be so send all your customers and clients a Bingo chip. Then tell them to go to your website and find out if they won the prize. You will have to put the winning chip's image on your website somewhere obscure so they have to search your site and get to know all your products and services, some they may not even be aware that you offer!

At the end of the month you can award the prize. Just make it valuable, and perhaps not even all from you. What about inviting other business owners to join you? They could each have a winning chip or you could have just one with a huge prize package. The ease and complexity is totally up to you. The important thing to remember is to make it fun for one and all.

Dec 3 Be a Blessing Day — Today we send kind good thoughts to everyone we touch. As you begin the busiest of season may I suggest the easiest way to be a blessing today to others is to share social media graphics. You'll find a few in Appendix A that you can brand and share.

Dec 5 Bathtub Party Day — Since soaking in a tub equals relaxing, tranquility, and "me time", may I suggest you focus on refreshing and renewal. It's time to show others how to make their lives less chaotic. This speaks to learning how to do something that would make their lives easier. If you happen to be the developer of apps that can do this, or train folks on how to focus their efforts in a more productive manner, this holiday is made just for you.

The rest of us could merely send real cards to our customers and clients or posting on social media. Tips and well wishes are the best way to accomplish your task while promoting your business.

Dec 5 "Irrational Exuberance" Day—Be happy that life is unpredictable as you celebrate today. Marking the 20th year since Allan Greenspan coined this phrase, we embrace the concept of being happy even when things are going against what we really wish they were. So, as you celebrate today remember the phrase, "Don't worry, be happy"? Well, today is a great time to follow that concept. You'll find a fun graphic you can use in Appendix A.

While everyone is scurrying about in preparation for the holiday, stress abounds, crowds are everywhere. Therefore, use this day to offer stress tips, or host a gathering to just have a little fun. Celebrate this day by sharing well wishes either with a real card, email, or social media post.

Dec 11 *United Nations: International Mountain Day— Mountains inspire us to always be strong. They motivate us stand tall against all our problems. Do you have things that are preventing you from achieving your dreams? Many of us do. So, as you think about ways to celebrate today, consider helping others overcome those obstacles. Events, tips, and techniques offered around this topic are the answers to these challenges. I have created a graphic that you can use on social media or print and hand out to others you meet today. You'll find it in Appendix A, and don't forget to brand it to your business.

Dec 21 Crossword Puzzle Day—It would probably surprise you to learn just how many people love crossword puzzles. And, if you can solve them, you not only increase your vocabulary and knowledge, but also your spelling too. So, as you think about how to celebrate today, any author or publisher, editor or speaking coach would do well to consider this the perfect day to host an event. Workshops or writing challenges would be in order, as well as would be public speaking training.

But to keep it simple, create your own crossword puzzle and share it. Use words that are pertinent to your business. Then post it on social media (or better yet your website for increased traffic, think SEO) and have those that can solve it give you their name and email address for a drawing. Remember to let them know you are going to be including them in future announcements so you can build your contact database. Furthermore, the answers to the clues could be taken right from your website, so that if they search around your site, they can find the answers.

At the very least, be sure to wish everyone you know a Happy Crossword Puzzle Day!

Appendix A: SAMPLES

Sample Press Release

FOR IMMEDIATE RELEASE
30+ YEAR LOCAL VETERAN BUSINESS OWNER / AUTHOR PARTNERS WITH PNC BANK
CLEARWATER, FL — SEPTEMBER 21, 2014

Local author and publisher, Ginger Marks, partners with Clearwater's PNC Bank to provide insight and advice for prospective, new, and experienced business owners. Ginger will be available to chat and sign copies of her award-winning book, Complete Library of Entrepreneurial Wisdom, and PNC Financial experts will be on hand to field your questions and educate you on business financial matters.

Mrs. Marks has spent 30+ years in the Tampa Bay area honing her skill as an entrepreneur. Having owned and operated multiple businesses, including a restaurant and a multimillion-dollar surgical clinic, she knows her way around business and how to operate one successfully.

Mrs. Marks states, "Owning a business takes many talents and the determination to succeed. In the course of my business operations I have experienced both the ups and the downs of the financial market. Without the knowledge of how to structure your finances to support your dreams you endanger your success. This is why I have partnered with PNC with the release of this important work."

Event date and location: October 9, 2014 between 5:30 and 6:30 pm at 2498 Gulf-to-Bay Blvd. Books available at your local bookstore and at this event.
# # #
MEDIA CONTACT: Ginger Marks, ginger.marks@documeantdesings.com 1-727-565-8500.

Glaucoma Awareness Handout

Risk Factors
- 50+ years old
- Severely nearsighted
- Family history
- High inter-ocular pressure
- History of eye trauma

Symptoms
- Increased inter-ocular pressure
- Blurred vision
- Eye redness
- Vision fatigue
- Eye and eyebrow pain
- Head pain
- Rainbow halo around light
- Teary eyed

Treatment
- Eye drops
- Good lighting
- Frequent rests while working, especially on computers
- Carbonic Anhydrase Inhibitors
- Anti-glaucoma eye glasses

Sponsored by:

Provided by: Company
address • city, state zip • phone • website

Dragon Facts

Characteristics
- Dominance
- Ambition
- Authority
- Dignity
- They prefer to live by their own rules and, if left on their own, are usually successful.
- They're driven, unafraid of challenges, and willing to take risks.

Dragon Movie Titles

Dinotopia

How to Train Your Dragon, How to Train Your Dragon 2, How to Train Your Dragon: The Hidden World

Dungeons and Dragons

Dragon Prince

George and the Dragon

The Hobbit; The Hobbit: There and Back Again; The Hobbit: The Battle of the Five Armies

Pete's Dragon

Reign of Fire

Dragonheart, Dragonheart: A New Beginning, Dragonheart 3: The Sorcerer's Curse

Fire and Ice

Dragon Hunters

Dragonslayer

Eragon

The Age of Dragons

The Mummy: Tomb of the Dragon Empire

Maleficent

Bewolf

Narna

Dragon to Movie Match Game
Use this list to create your own Dragon to Movie Match Game

Bix, Brokenhorn, Stinktooth: Dinotopia

Smite: George and the Dragon

Darksmoke: Adventures of a Teenage Dragon Slayer

Alina: Beyond Sherwood Forest

Bio Dragon: Dragonfighter

Dagahra: Rebirth of Mothra II

Diavai: Maleficent

Draco: Dragonheart, Dragonheart: A New Beginning, Dragonheart 3: The Sorcerer's Curse

Elliott: Pete's Dragon

Falazure: Dragon God

Falkor: The Neverending Story, The NeverEnding Story II: The Next Chapter, The NeverEnding Story III: Escape from Fantasia

Fire and ice dragons: Dragonquest

Hydra: Hercules, Jason and the Argonauts, Percy Jackson & the Olympians: The Lightning Thief

Jabberwocky: Alice in Wonderland, Alice Through the Looking Glass

Norbert(a) Norwegian Ridgeback, Hungarian Horntail, Ukrainian Ironbelly; Harry Potter Series

Olly: Stanley's Dragon

Orochimaru; The Magic Serpent

Pendragon: Jack the Giant Killer

Smaug: The Hobbit

Queen Narissa: Enchanted

Vermithrax Pejorative: Dragonslayer

Yowler: Dragonworld

Appendix A: SAMPLES | 67

Birdseed Package

Trim size: 3.75 by 3.25 inches.

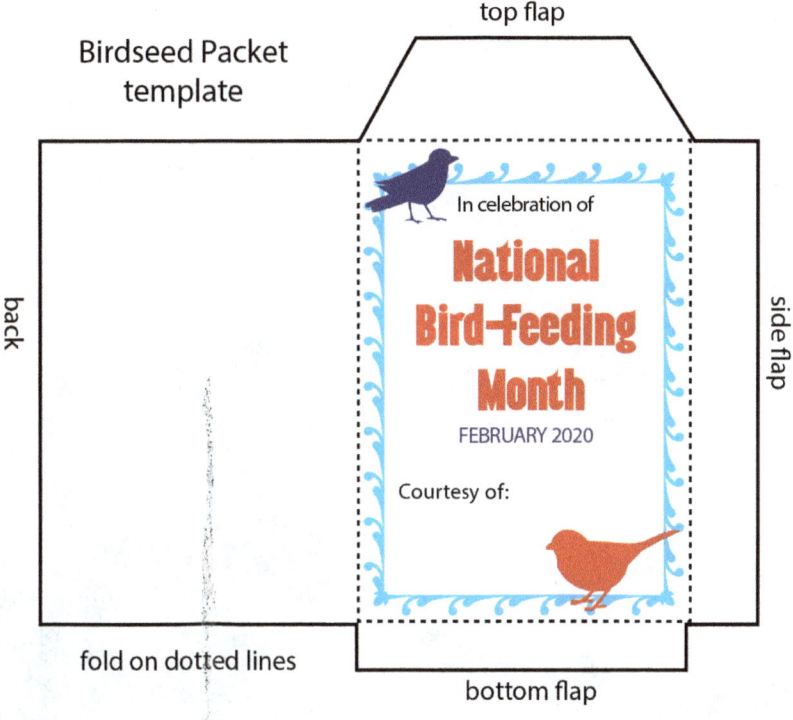

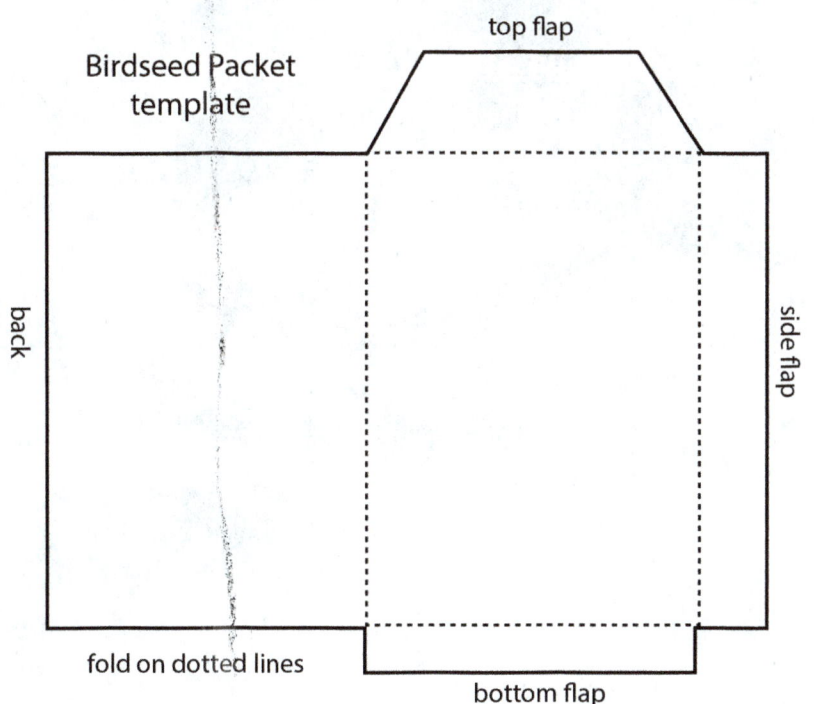

Dracula Day Event Flyer

Words Matter Week Card

Words Matter Social Media Graphic

World Poetry Day Graphic

Silence

In quite contemplation I sit and wonder,
Amazed at the world that reveals itself daily.

Could what is around the next bend,
lead to romance and fame,
or will life pass me by,
only time will tell.

But if I take control
and don't let it fly,
life will be full and
never dare to pass me by.

Ginger Marks

[Your Company]
wishes you a day filled
with prose.

March 21, 2020
United Nations: World Poetry Day

World Poetry Day Infographic

For the full-size version or if you need help customizing it to your business brand contact Ginger at ginger.marks@documeantdesigns.com.

7 TYPES OF POETRY

HAIKU — Traditionally, haiku poems are three-line stanzas with a 5/7/5 syllable count. It focuses on the beauty and simplicity found in nature. As its popularity grew, the 5/7/5 formula has often been broken. However, the focus remains the same—simple moments in life.

FREE VERSE — The least defined. In fact, they're deliberately irregular, taking on an improvisational bent. There's no formula, no pattern. Rather, the writer and reader must work together to set the speed, intonation, and emotional pull.

CINQUAINS — A five-line poem inspired by the Japanese haiku. There are many different variations of cinquain including American cinquains, didactic cinquains, reverse cinquains, butterfly cinquains, and crown cinquains.

EPIC — A long and narrative poem that normally tells a story about a hero or an adventure. Epics can be presented as oral or written stories.

BALLAD — Also tells a story, like epic poems do. However, ballad poetry is often based on a legend or a folk tale. These poems may take the form of songs, or they may contain a moral or a lesson.

ACROSTIC — Also known as name poems, spell out names or words with the first letter in each line. While the author is doing this, they're describing someone or something they deem important.

SONNETS — Sonetto is actually Italian for "a little sound or song." This form has grabbed poets by the heart for centuries. It began as a 14-line poem written in iambic pentameter. Although flourishes have been made over time, the general principle remains the same.

Mar 21, 2020 United Nations World Poetry Day

Courtesy of:

Pony Express Game

Courtesy of Boy Scout Trail
https://boyscouttrail.com/content/game/pony_express_relay-2148.asp

The pony express was a relay to get mail, magazines, and messages through to their destination before even the telegraph and railroad existed. So, a relay game seems a fit game for your Pony Express day event. You might even want to create an online version if you have the imagination to do so.

Required:

A selection of old letters, envelopes, newspapers — about 6 per patrol.

Preparation:

Mark a starting line and a distant turning spot, about 20 to 50 feet away, depending on space.

Place the mailbag about 15 feet behind the starting line, or some other place out of the way.

Instructions:

Pony Express riders were fast and fearless. They would ride into a station and leap from their spent horse onto a fresh one to continue their long journey delivering important mail.

Patrols line up.

One scout on each patrol is chosen to be the Pony Express Rider.

All the rest are horses.

On 'Go', all riders run to the mailbag and grab one letter to carry.

They then return to their patrol and mount a fresh horse. They set out to the far marker and back.

When riders reach their patrol, they switch from the tired horse to a fresh one for another ride.

Riders that touch the ground, at any point along the course, must run to the mailbag and retrieve another letter to carry while the horse rests.

Riders that touch the ground when switching horses must retrieve two letters.

Letters accumulate and need to be delivered at the end of the line.

First patrol to complete a predefined number of laps is the winner.

If played outside, set up a large oval course with 3 or 4 switching stations spaced around it and the mailbag in the center. The first patrol to complete a certain number of laps is the winner.

Chili Recipes

Best Damn Chili by Danny Jaye

Ingredients

4 tablespoons olive oil
1 yellow onion, chopped
1 red bell pepper, chopped
1 Anaheim chile pepper, chopped
2 red jalapeno pepper, chopped
4 garlic cloves, minced
2 1/2 pounds lean ground beef
1/4 cup Worcestershire sauce
1 pinch garlic powder, or to taste
2 beef bouillon cubes
1 (12 fluid ounce) can or bottle light beer (such as Coors(R))
1 (28 ounce) can crushed San Marzano tomatoes
1 (14.5 ounce) can fire-roasted diced tomatoes
1 (12 ounce) can tomato paste
1/2 cup white wine
2 tablespoons chili powder
2 tablespoons ground cumin
1 tablespoon brown sugar
1 tablespoon chipotle pepper sauce
2 1/2 teaspoons dried basil
1 1/2 teaspoons smoked paprika
1 teaspoon salt
1/2 teaspoon dried oregano
1/2 teaspoon ground black pepper
2 (16 ounce) cans dark red kidney beans (such as Bush's(R))
1 cup sour cream
3 tablespoons chopped fresh cilantro
1/2 teaspoon ground cumin

Directions

Heat oil in a large pot over medium heat; cook and stir onion, bell pepper, Anaheim pepper, jalapeno peppers, and garlic in the hot oil until softened.

Meanwhile, heat a large skillet over medium-high heat. Cook and stir beef in the hot skillet until browned and crumbly, 5 to 7 minutes; add Worcestershire sauce and garlic powder. Crumble bouillon cubes over beef and add beer. Continue to cook, scraping any browned bits from the bottom of the skillet, until liquid is hot, about 3 minutes. Stir beef mixture into pepper mixture.

Stir crushed tomatoes, diced tomatoes, tomato paste, and wine to the beef mixture. Season with chili powder, 2 tablespoons cumin, brown sugar, pepper sauce, basil, paprika, salt, oregano, and black pepper. Bring to a boil and reduce heat to medium-low. Cover and simmer until meat and vegetables are very tender and flavors have developed in the chili, about 90 minutes, stirring occasionally.

Mix kidney beans into beef and vegetables. Continue to simmer until beans are hot, about 30 minutes more.

Blend sour cream, cilantro, and remaining 1/2 teaspoon cumin in a food processor until smooth. Serve sour cream mixture with chili.

ALL RIGHTS RESERVED © 2019 Allrecipes.com

Keith's White Chicken Chili

Ingredients

2 cups diced onions
2 cups diced celery
5 garlic cloves, chopped
1/2 cup vegetable oil
1-pound chicken breast, cooked and diced
8 cups water
1 bay leaf
1 (7-ounce) can chopped green chilies
1/2 teaspoon oregano
1/2 teaspoon cumin
1/2 teaspoon dry mustard
1/2 teaspoon basil
1/2 teaspoon Old Bay seasoning
1/4 teaspoon Cajun seasoning
1/3 of a 7-ounce can chipotle in adobo, chopped
4 tablespoons chicken base
1 pickled jalapeno, chopped
2 pounds white beans, soaked overnight
1/2 cup heavy cream
1 cup shredded carrots
16 ounces sour cream

Directions

Sauté onion, celery, and garlic in oil until tender, about 5 minutes. In a large stockpot add chicken, water, bay leaf, chiles, oregano, cumin, dry mustard, basil, Old Bay, Cajun seasoning, chipotle, chicken base, and pickled jalapeno and simmer for 1 1/2 hours. Add the drained beans and heavy cream and simmer for 1 hour, or until the beans are tender. Garnish soup with carrots and sour cream.

This recipe was provided by professional chefs and has been scaled down from a bulk recipe provided by a restaurant. The Food Network chefs have not tested this recipe, in the proportions indicated, and therefore, we cannot make any representation as to the results.

Episode#: BE1E09
Copyright © 2003 Television Food Network, G.P., All Rights Reserved

Michelle's Basic Chili

Ingredients

2 pounds ground beef
2 onions, chopped
4 cloves garlic, minced
2 tablespoons chili powder
2 teaspoons salt
2 teaspoons dried oregano
4 (14.5 ounce) cans stewed tomatoes
1 (15 ounce) can tomato sauce
1 (15 ounce) can kidney beans with liquid

Directions

Combine ground beef, onion, and garlic in large stockpot. Cook and stir over medium heat until beef is brown. Drain.

Stir in chili powder, salt, oregano, tomatoes, and tomato sauce; break up tomatoes while stirring. Heat to boiling, reduce heat to simmer, and cover. Cook, stirring occasionally, for 1 hour.

Stir in beans. Simmer, uncovered, for 20 minutes; stir occasionally.

ALL RIGHTS RESERVED © 2019 Allrecipes.com

Holly's Best Chili Recipe

Ingredients

2 pounds lean ground beef
1 onion diced
1 jalapeno seeded and finely diced
4 cloves garlic minced
2 1/2 tablespoons chili powder divided (or to taste)
1 teaspoon cumin
1 green bell pepper seeded and diced
14.5 oz crushed tomatoes canned
19 oz kidney beans canned, drained & rinsed
14.5 oz diced tomatoes with juice
1 1/2 cups beef broth
1 cup beer
1 tablespoon tomato paste
1 tablespoon brown sugar optional
salt and pepper to taste

Directions

Combine ground beef and 1 1/2 tablespoons chili powder.

In a large pot, brown ground beef, onion, jalapeno, and garlic. Drain any fat.

Add in remaining ingredients and bring to a boil. Reduce heat and simmer uncovered 45-60 minutes or until chili has reached desired thickness.

Top with cheddar cheese, green onions, cilantro or other favorite toppings.

© SpendWithPennies.com. Content and photographs are copyright protected.

Beaver Facts

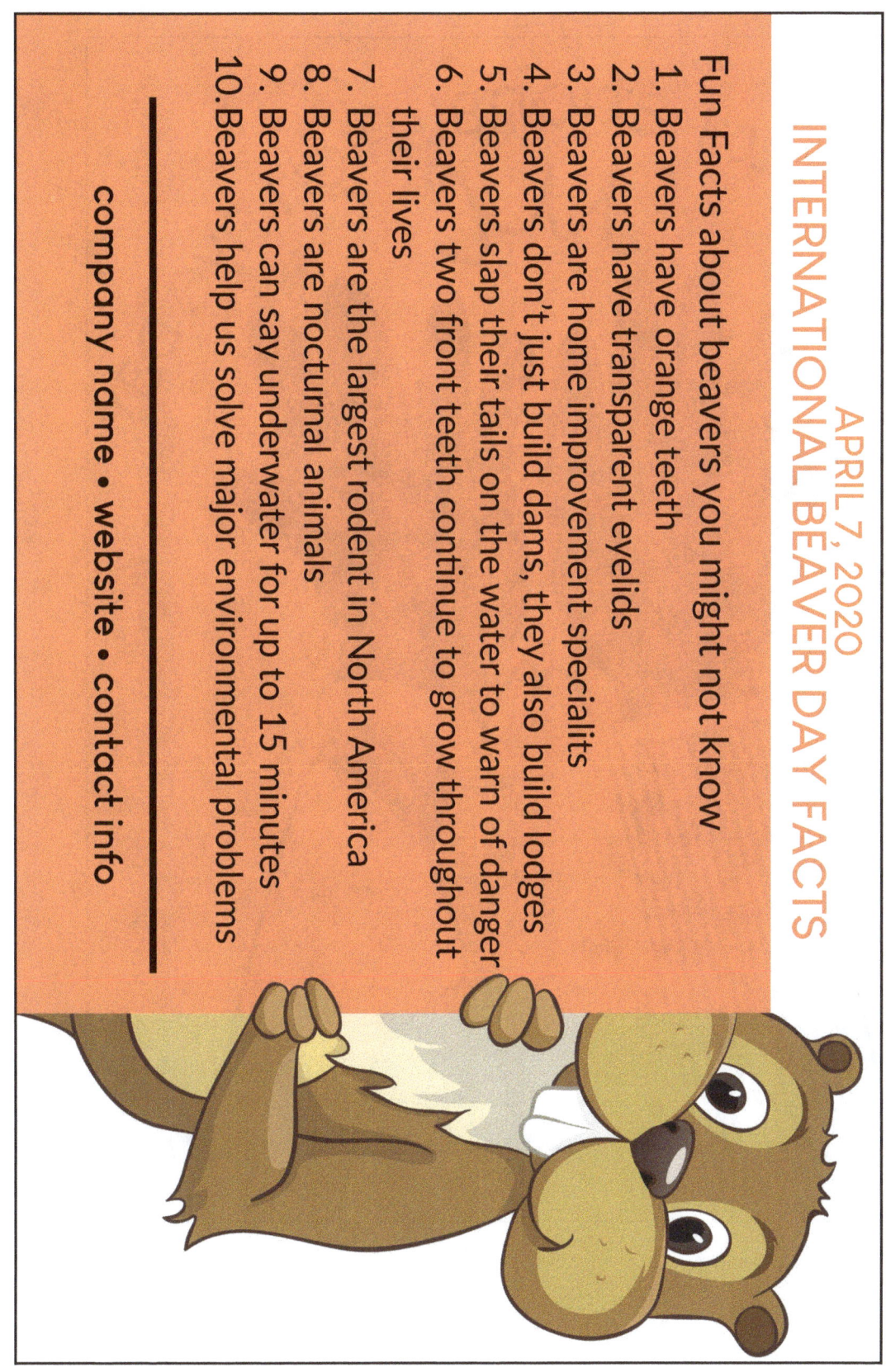

APRIL 7, 2020
INTERNATIONAL BEAVER DAY FACTS

Fun Facts about beavers you might not know

1. Beavers have orange teeth
2. Beavers have transparent eyelids
3. Beavers are home improvement specialits
4. Beavers don't just build dams, they also build lodges
5. Beavers slap their tails on the water to warn of danger
6. Beavers two front teeth continue to grow throughout their lives
7. Beavers are the largest rodent in North America
8. Beavers are nocturnal animals
9. Beavers can say underwater for up to 15 minutes
10. Beavers help us solve major environmental problems

company name • website • contact info

National High Five Day Graphic

New Friends Old Friends Week Graphics

International New Friends Old Friends Week

May 17–23, 2020

company • website

Respect for Chickens Day Poster

Respect for Chickens Day Poster

Respect for Chickens Day Button

Sock Drive Flyer

Towel Day Button

How To Organize a Clothes Drive

Courtesy of Goodnet.org

The key to making sure that your clothes drive will have maximum impact is a two-pronged effort spread out over the planning phase, and then the event itself. With this handy guide, you'll be a charity pro in no time.

1. FIND A LOCAL PARTNER

Before you start collecting a ton of things that people might not even need, get in touch with a local homeless shelter, Goodwill, the Salvation Army, The National Coalition for the Homeless and/or The National Coalition for Homeless Veterans. These organizations have years of experience and know exactly what the community they serve needs.

2. BUILD A TEAM

The more people you will have to help you the bigger the success of your drive will be. Talk to your family, friends, colleagues, faith group members, or book club devotees to join your effort. Together you can come up with the perfect project and some of the new team members you just won may even have prior experience doing these kinds of things.

3. SET YOUR GOAL

Setting a goal gives you something concrete to strive for and helps to hold yourself accountable. Commit as an individual as well as a team to collecting a specific number of boxes and reaching out to a certain number of people. Aim high and remain flexible in case you remain short or overshoot your goals. Choose one member of your team to update the others on the progress you are making to keep the spirits high.

4. IDENTIFY A DROP-OFF LOCATION AND A TIMEFRAME

The collection location for your drive could be anything from an office, apartment building or even your garage. Anything that will allow lots of people to come by and you to store (hopefully) lots of boxes for a while. Decide on collection days—you don't want to limit potential donors to just one day—and your team will need at least a few days to sort through all the donations.

5. GET THE WORD OUT

Spread the word on as many different channels as you can. Social media is a wonderful medium, but don't forego good old-fashioned flyers and posters which you can hand out and pin to message boards at work or church. If you have tech-savvy team members, you can even make a website or register your drive on Serve.gov.

6. SORT INCOMING DONATIONS

As soon as those donations start coming in, begin pre-sorting everything so you won't be faced with a mountain of work once you finish your drive. You can sort clothes into children's clothes, female, male and misc. (blankets, socks, bed sheets etc), or according to what different organizations you contacted told you they will need. Pack everything in clean boxes or bags to make delivery easier.

7. DELIVER YOUR DONATIONS

Now that everything is packed and sorted, it's time for your team to celebrate by delivering the fruit of your labor to its destination. Some NGO's are able to send trucks to pick up donations, but most will need you to rent a van and to the delivery.

8. SHARE YOUR SUCCESS STORY

Be sure to document everything with lots of photos which you can share on social media to motivate others to follow in your footsteps. If you collected email addresses from donors, this is a good chance to send a Thank-You-mail to let everyone see the impact their donations made.

Upsy Daisy Day Graphic

88 | 2020 Weird & Wacky Holiday Marketing Guide

Asteroid Template

Directions: Cut, fold, and glue.

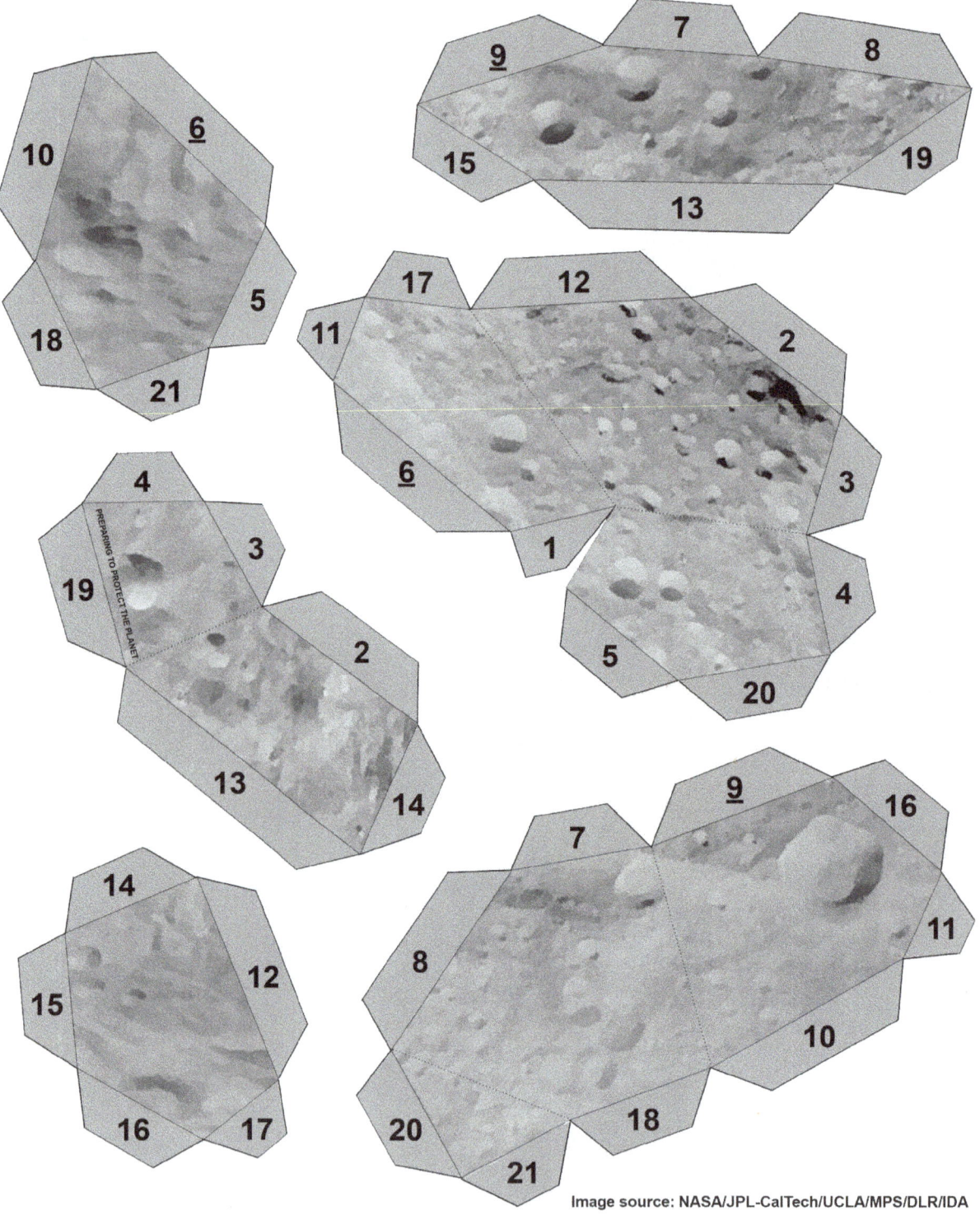

Image source: NASA/JPL-CalTech/UCLA/MPS/DLR/IDA

Globe Template

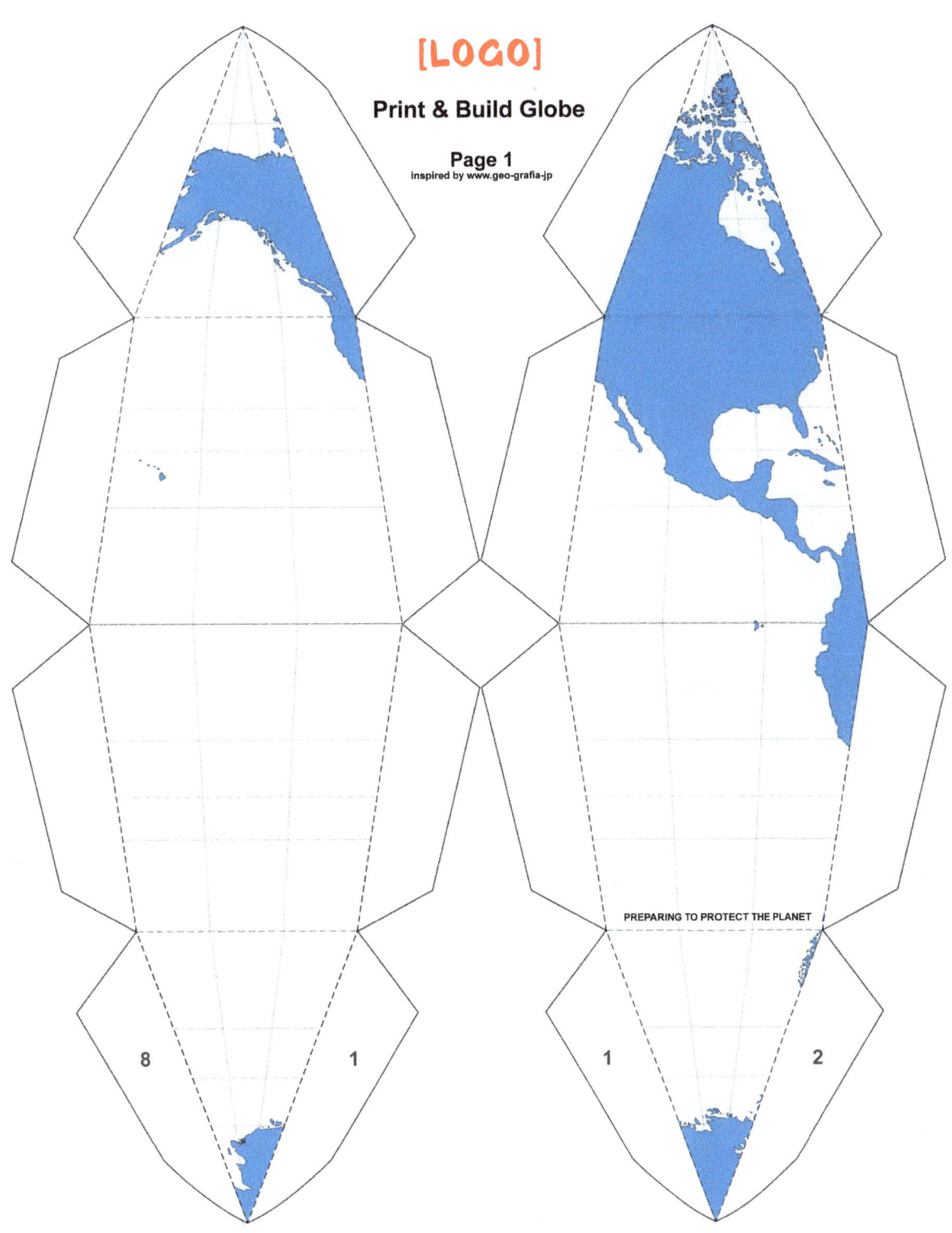

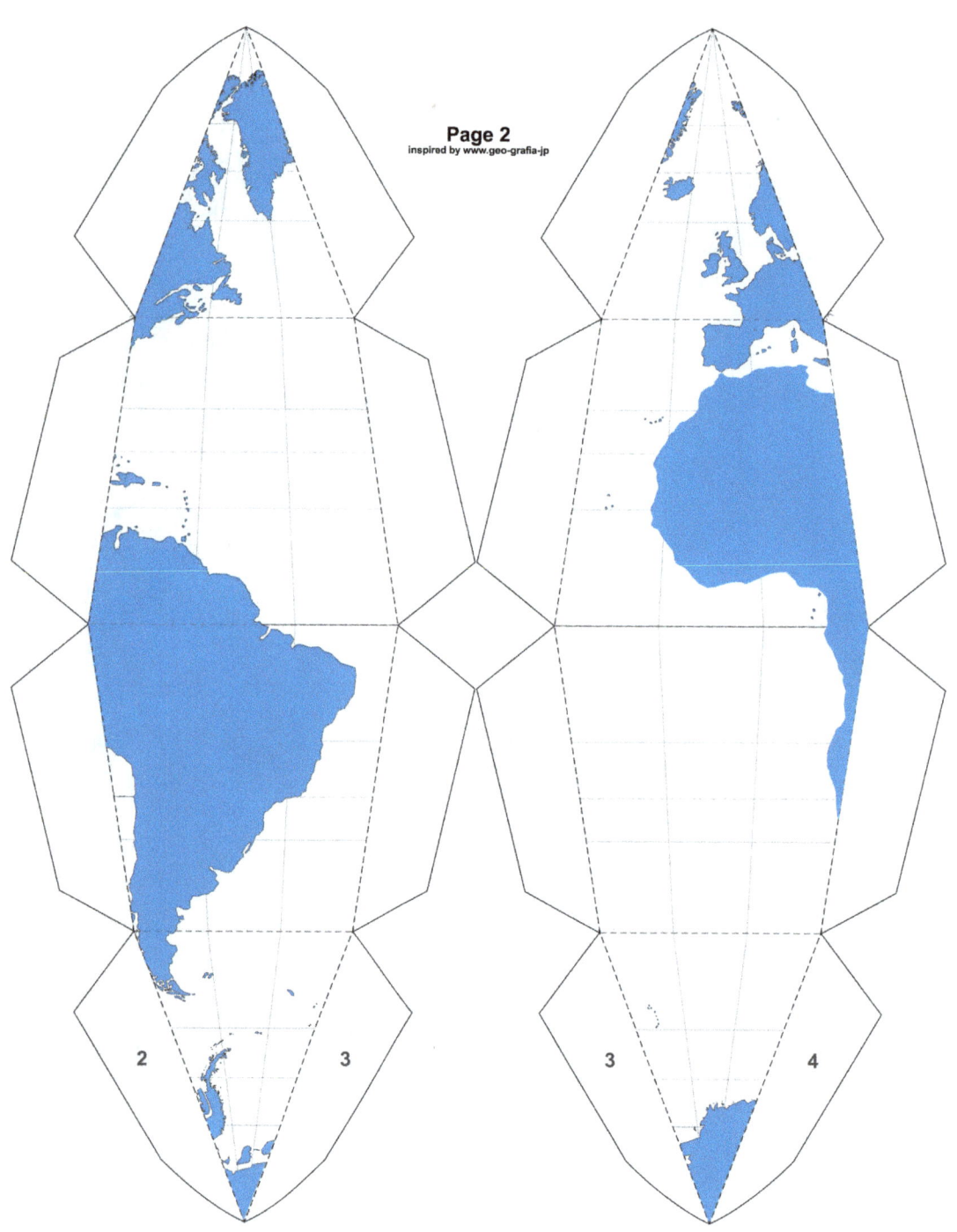

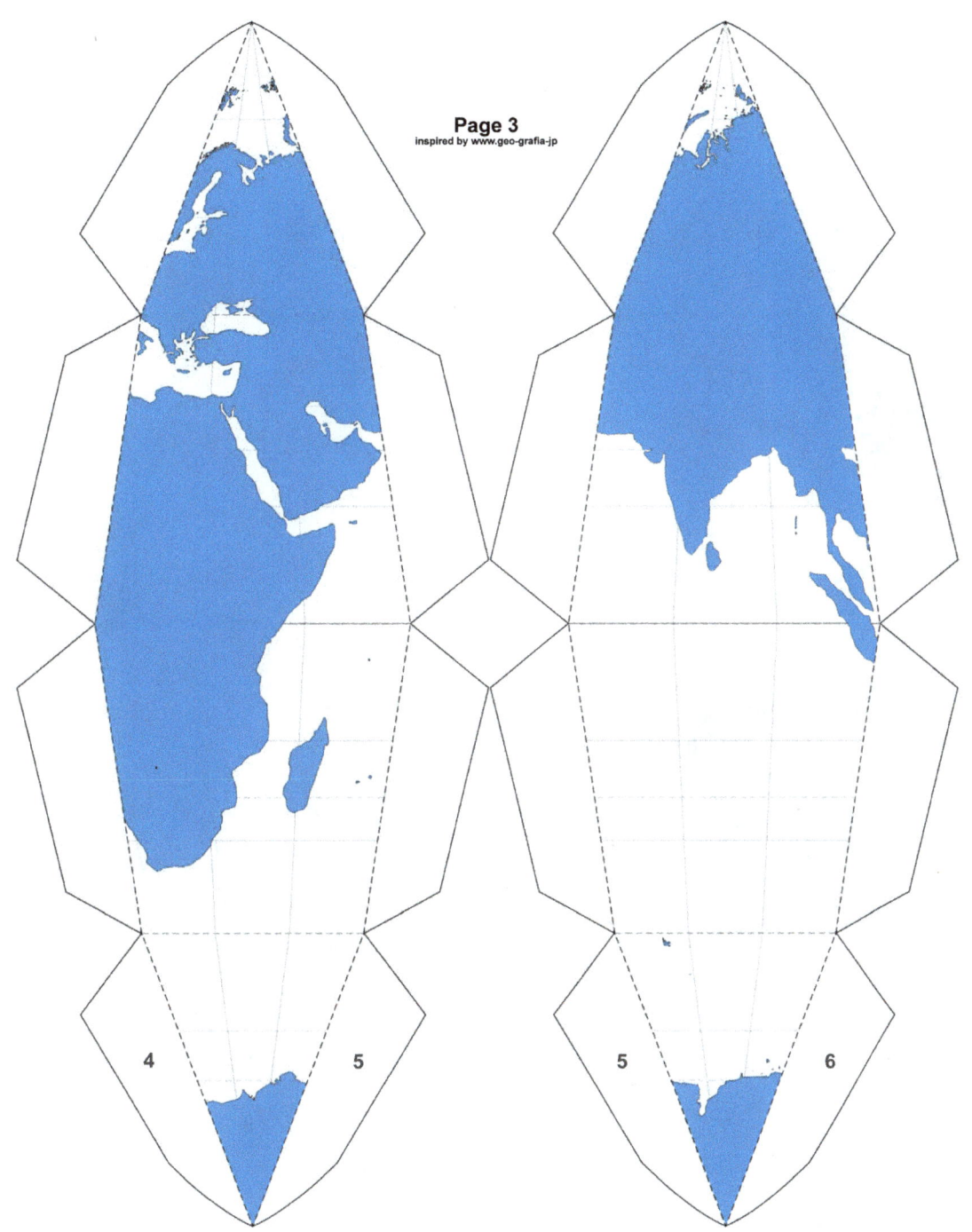

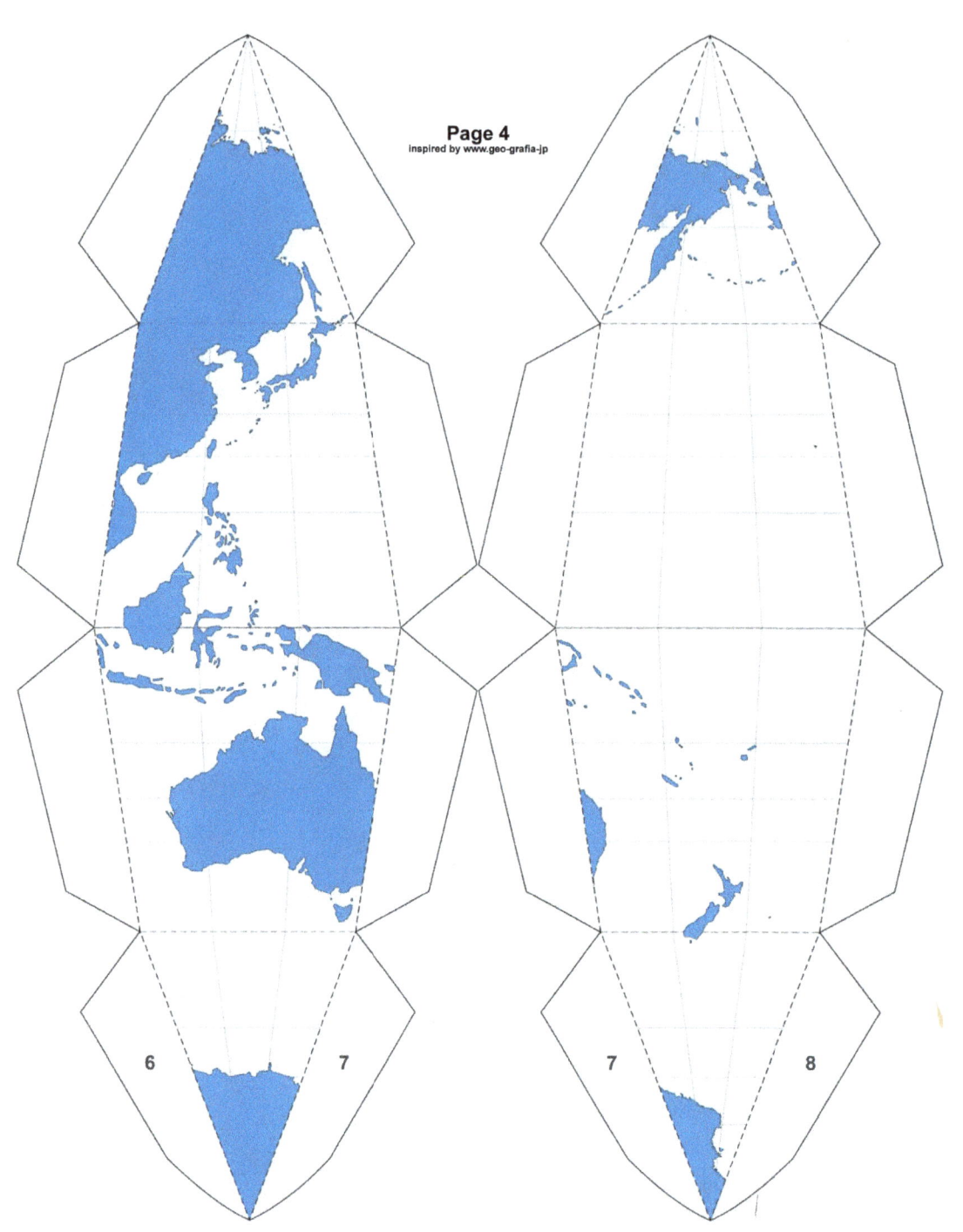

Sports Clichés*

Sports clichés used in business

According to Don R. Powell, licensed psychologist and president of the American Institute for Preventive Medicine, sports clichés are used in about 50 percent of corporate boardrooms. They provide a shorthand to quickly communicate ideas. According to Powell, "We have a love/hate relationship with cliches. Although we complain about them, we are enamored with them. That's because they always seem to fit." [1]

- "It was a slam dunk."
- "It's gut-check time." [1]
- "Keep your eye on the ball." [2] [3]
- "Monday-Morning Quarterback"
- "That was a hole in one."
- "They don't pull any punches." [1]
- "They dropped the ball." [1]
- "They always step up to the plate." [1]
- "They talk a good game." [1]
- "They're a team player." [1]
- "They're in a league of their own." [1]
- "They want to play hardball." [1]
- "The ball's in your court." [1]
- "They answered the bell." [1]
- "We knocked it out of the park."
- "Take one for the team"
- "Offense sells tickets, defense wins championships"

Sports clichés used in sports announcing

- "A 2–0 lead is the worst lead"
- "Alligator arms" [4]
- "They have to have a great game for their team to win." [4]
- "They have to get on the same page." [4]
- "The media are blowing this out of proportion." [4]
- "That will come back to haunt them." [4]
- "I'd like to thank my Lord and savior." [4]
- "Throw under the bus." [4]
- "D-Line or O-Line." [4]

- "A lot of open looks at the basket." [4]
- "It doesn't get any better than this." [4]
- "He's a warrior." [4]
- "Defense wins championships." [4]
- "The best defense is a good offense." [4]
- "Midfield maestro" is a term used in association football to describe a midfield player who excels in the technical and creative aspects of midfield play and who often create goalscoring opportunities for the attackers, while at the same time controlling the tempo of the match and raising the game of the other members of the team. [5]
- "Charity Stripe"
- "Goals are not deserved, goals are made"
- "On any given Sunday..."
- "Play one game at a time"
- "There is no 'I' in 'team'"
- "There ain't no 'U' either" — as a retort to "There is no 'I' in 'team'"

Sports film clichés

- A down and out coach is offered one last shot.[6]
- The coach can't get along with his star player.[6]
- Someone doubts the protagonist's abilities, and is made to believe in them.[6]
- The players overcome race relations or gang violence, and are brought together by being a team.[6]
- The opposing team is larger, better dressed, better equipped yet end up defeated by the protagonist's team.[6]
- A death or injury provides the main character with the extra incentive to win.[6]
- The main character is considered too old to win, yet does.[6]
- An emotional speech inspires the protagonists.[6]
- Near the end of the movie it will seem that the protagonist's team has no chance of winning, but they quickly bounce back with little time left.
- The protagonist's team makes a valiant comeback effort only to fall just short at the last second (Puck hits the post, shot rims out, etc.). This is immediately followed by a dramatic montage with tear soaked hugs of players and coaches who are genuinely better off for the experience.
- After a supreme achievement on the sports field/court/diamond, the achiever will, for no apparent reason, extend his arm and use his forefinger to point, for an extended period of time, to a team-mate, coach or even someone in the crowd. In many cases, the person being pointed to will, inexplicably, return the gesture.

References

Athletes' Day-to-Day Drivel https://web.archive.org/web/20070929122212/http://www2.jsonline.com/sports/net/nov00/net111400.asp

Caught on the Web: Pittsburgh Post-Gazette http://www.postgazette.com/sports/other/20010918caught0919ap6.asp

Note to Copy Editors http://www.spokesmanreview.com/library/siteseeing/siteseeing.asp?ID=011209

[1] "Sports Cliches Go from Locker Room to Boardroom". KUSI News. Archived from the original on September 27, 2007. Retrieved 2007-03-14.

[2] "keep your eye on the ball". keep eye on the ball. Farlex. Retrieved 26 December 2012.

[3] Reynolds, Gretchen (28 November 2012). "Keeping Your Eye on the Ball". NY Times. Retrieved 26 December 2012.

[4] "Sportscasters: Ditch the cliches". USA Today. 2006-12-22. Retrieved 2007-03-14.

[5] Tom Bellwood (2009-10-01). "THE LIST: Football's best midfield maestros — The top 10 | Mail Online". Dailymail.co.uk. Retrieved 2013-12-17.

[6] "The enduring, lovable sports-film clichés". Today.com. Retrieved 2007-03-14.

*A more extensive list can be found at http://www.sportscliche.com/

Sports Cliché Week Buttons

July 12–18, 2020 Sports Cliché Week

company • URL

When it stops being fun, it's time to quit.

[logo]   July 12–18, 2020
Sports Cliché Week

National Watermelon Day Graphic

Appendix A: SAMPLES | 101

Be an Angel Day Random Act of Kindness (RAK) Cards

Fall Hat Month Social Media Graphic

Fall Hat Month Clothing Drive

Fall Hat Month Event Flyer

September
Fall Hat Month

sponsored by: company • URL

Event Details

List of Misused Words & Phrases

Affect: The result of something done or applied. Effect: The cause of the affect.

Chose: Past tense of the action of choosing. Choose: Present tense of the action of choosing.

Lie: To recline; does not require an object. Lay: To put something down; requires and object.

Principal vs. Principle. Your pal is the principal, but his principle job is to keep the school running smoothly.

"Hear, hear." Not "Here, here."

"Et cetera" should be shortened to etc. and always end it with a period. Latin for "and the rest." 'Et alia' is shortened to et al. and again always end it with a period. Latin for "and others."

"Rein it in", not reign it in. A rein is a tether, while reign is what a monarch does over a serf.

"In regard to." Not 'In regards to." Could also be with regard to.

"You and me" or "You and I." Always put the other person first. As for which to use me or I, try reading the sentence without the other person in it. If is sound off, then it is wrong. Example: "George and me went to the movies." Read without George: "Me went to the movies." This is incorrect. So, the proper grammar is "George and I went to the movies."

Cite: To quote someone or something.

Site: A location.

Sight: What you use your eyes for.

Could have/Should have. Not could of or should of.

"Couldn't care less." Not "Could care less." If you 'could' then you are capable of caring less.

"Enamored of" not "enamored by". By indicated the other thing or person is being enamored. So, if that's not the case and it is you being enamored, then you are "enamored of."

Flesh out: To add substance.

Flush out: To bring out of hiding

Gibe vs. Jive or Jibe. If your ideas don't come together with other people's ideas then they don't jibe. Jive is used as an affect of the jibe. Gibe is a joke or tease.

Queue vs Cue: Queue is putting in order whereas cue is what you give to an actor.

"Toe the line". Not, "Tow the line." This refers to a stepping over a proverbial or imaginary line, like in the sand. Your physical toe would do that. So, it should be 'toe' not 'tow'.

Adverse vs. Averse: Adverse means bad like having a bad reaction to a medication. While being averse to something means not wanting to participate, or in disagreement.

"Home in" vs. "Hone in". To hone is to sharpen, so you would not hone in, you would come closer to the mark by homing in on the object.

"Champing at the bit". Not "Chomping at the bit". Champing means to chew or bite loudly. It is what horses do to their bit and where the phrase originated.

Fewer vs. Less. Fewer is a number, while less is a quantity.

9x13 Day Graphic

wishing you a happy
9x13 Day
company • URL

Tradesman Day Infographic

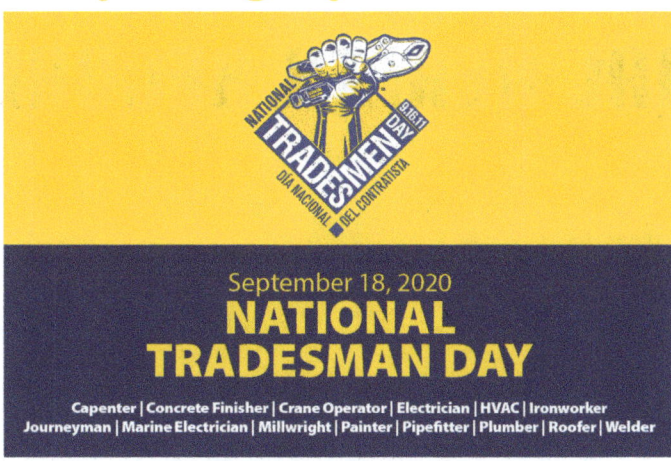

Medical Records Organizational Tabs

PERSONAL HEALTH RECORD (PHR)

Name:

Date of Birth:

Blood Type :

Chronic Health Issues:

Allergies & Reactions: (including drug or food allergies)

Children & DOBs:

Emergency Healthcare Information: (e.g., a pacemaker, stent or hearing and vision problems)

CONTENTS

Personal Information
Medical Records
    Advanced Directives
    Immunizations
    Test Results
    Hospitalizations
    Vision
    Hearing
    Dental
Medical History
Prescriptions / Vitamins / Supplements
    Past
    Present
Doctor Office Visits (date, doctor name, and notes)
Major Health Concerns
    Past
    Present
Family Medical History
Insurance
    Bills / Receipts
    Conversation Log
Important Contact Information
    Physicians
    Pharmacy
    Insurance
    Family
    Surrogate

MEDICAL RECORDS

Organize medical history and current health information categorically and chronologically.

Advanced Directives (living will & healthcare power of attorney)

Immunizations

Test Results

Hospitalizations

Vision

Hearing

Dental

MEDICAL HISTORY

List of current and past supplements, prescriptions, and over-the-counter medications. Write down the drug name, dosage, start date, end date, and the condition it is treating, plus any side effects experienced.

Prescriptions

    Past

    Present

Vitamins / Supplements

Doctor office visits (date, doctor name, and notes)

Major Health Concerns

    Past

    Present

Family Medical History

INSURANCE

Log of phone conversations with insurance representatives, including the date and name of the person you spoke with. Include a copy of your insurance and Medicare card.

Bills/Receipts

Conversation Log

IMPORTANT CONTACTS

Record names, medical practices, addresses, telephone numbers, and email (if applicable) of your doctors and pharmacist. Include the emergency contact information of a caregiver, family member, or friend in case of an emergency. Include the name, policy number, address, and telephone number of your health insurance company.

Physicians

Pharmacy

Insurance

Family

Health Surrogate

Wallet-Sized Medication Card

Medication Card

Name:

Date of Birth:

Emergency Contact:

Emergency Contact Phone:

What medications should I include?
- Prescription medicines
- Over-the-Counter medicines
- Vitamins
- Herbal remedies
- Nutrition pills
- Respiratory therapy medicines (inhalers)
- Blood factors (such as Factor VIII)
- IV solutions
- IV nutrition
- Patches
- Eye or ear drops
- Cremes
- Ointments

Other important information

DATE THIS FORM LAST UPDATED: _____

Allergies and reactions (include: food, drug, latex, environmental)

Start Date	Drug Name	Strength	Dosage (pills, units, puffs, drops)	Route	When do you take this medicine? (How many times a day? Morning & night? After meals?)	Reason — Why do you take this medicine?

provided by: company • URL

Business Card-Sized Medication Card

Name _____ Date _____	Name _____ Date _____
Medication _____ Dosage _____	Medication _____ Dosage _____
Medication _____ Dosage _____	Medication _____ Dosage _____
Medication _____ Dosage _____	Medication _____ Dosage _____
Medication _____ Dosage _____	Medication _____ Dosage _____
Medication _____ Dosage _____	Medication _____ Dosage _____
Medication _____ Dosage _____	Medication _____ Dosage _____

Medication _____ Dosage _____	Medication _____ Dosage _____
Medication _____ Dosage _____	Medication _____ Dosage _____
Medication _____ Dosage _____	Medication _____ Dosage _____
Medication _____ Dosage _____	Medication _____ Dosage _____
Medication _____ Dosage _____	Medication _____ Dosage _____
Allergy _____ Reaction _____	Allergy _____ Reaction _____
Allergy _____ Reaction _____	Allergy _____ Reaction _____
courtesy of:	courtesy of:

Name _____ Date _____	Name _____ Date _____
Medication _____ Dosage _____	Medication _____ Dosage _____
Medication _____ Dosage _____	Medication _____ Dosage _____
Medication _____ Dosage _____	Medication _____ Dosage _____
Medication _____ Dosage _____	Medication _____ Dosage _____
Medication _____ Dosage _____	Medication _____ Dosage _____
Medication _____ Dosage _____	Medication _____ Dosage _____

Medication _____ Dosage _____	Medication _____ Dosage _____
Medication _____ Dosage _____	Medication _____ Dosage _____
Medication _____ Dosage _____	Medication _____ Dosage _____
Medication _____ Dosage _____	Medication _____ Dosage _____
Medication _____ Dosage _____	Medication _____ Dosage _____
Allergy _____ Reaction _____	Allergy _____ Reaction _____
Allergy _____ Reaction _____	Allergy _____ Reaction _____
courtesy of:	courtesy of:

National Kick Butt Day Graphic

Appendix A: SAMPLES | 117

International Evaluate Your Life Day Graphic

Personal SWOT Analysis

Courtesy of Mind Tools

Personal SWOT Analysis Worksheet

- For instructions on using Personal SWOT Analysis, visit www.mindtools.com/personalswot.

Strengths	**Weaknesses**
What do you do well? What unique resources can you draw on? What do others see as your strengths?	What could you improve? Where do you have fewer resources than others? What are others likely to see as weaknesses?
Opportunities	**Threats**
What opportunities are open to you? What trends could you take advantage of? How can you turn your strengths into opportunities?	What threats could harm you? What is your competition doing? What threats do your weaknesses expose you to?

© Copyright Mind Tools Ltd, 2006-2017.
Please feel free to copy this sheet for your own use and to share with friends, co-workers or team members, just as long as you do not change it in any way.

Organ Donation Infographic

Courtesy of Piedmont.com (https://www.piedmont.org/living-better/infographic-organ-donation-saves-lives)

ORGAN DONATION SAVES LIVES

In my 14 years of experience in organ transplantation, I have seen nearly 2,000 lives saved by the generosity of organ donors. I have also seen the suffering patients and their families go through when the call for a transplant never comes. The most critical step in the entire transplant process is the first: when a donor first signs their driver's license and tells their family they'd like to be an organ donor.

Jon Hundley, M.D.,
Piedmont Transplant Institute surgeon

ORGAN & TISSUE DONATION FACTS

21 People die each day awaiting a transplant.

ONE organ donor can save EIGHT lives.

Every 10 MINUTES, someone is added to the transplant waiting list.

ONE tissue donor can enhance the lives of **50+** people.

Every **10 MINUTES**, someone is added to the transplant waiting list.

$0 Cost to donors or their families

Some diseases of the kidneys, heart, lungs, pancreas and liver are **FOUND MORE FREQUENTLY IN MINORITY POPULATIONS.**

Greater diversity of donors

Increased chance of a match

People from these populations have a particularly **HIGH NEED FOR ORGAN TRANSPLANTS.**

Compatible **BLOOD TYPES** and **TISSUE MARKERS** are critical qualities for donor and recipient matching.

IMPROVED SURVIVAL RATES

God gave me a second chance at life when I had my liver transplant, so I need to live life to the fullest. It is my mission to raise awareness among people of color about the need for and importance of organ donation.

Mia Portis
Liver transplant recipient, Piedmont Transplant Institute

FACT Deceased donor kidney recipients live about *twice as long* as they would have on dialysis.

FACT Living donor kidney recipients fare even better. Living donor kidneys last *twice as long* as deceased donor kidneys.

75% **FIVE-YEAR SURVIVAL RATE** for liver transplant recipients.

WHAT CAN BE DONATED?

WHAT CAN BE DONATED?

ORGANS

 Kidneys*  Heart

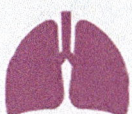 Lungs*  Liver*

 Pancreas*  Intestines*

*A living individual can donate a kidney, and parts of the pancreas, lung, liver, or intestine.

TISSUE

 Veins  Corneas  Heart Valves   Middle Ear

 Bone  Skin  Cartilage  Tendons

 Ligaments

Each year, more than **1.5 MILLION PEOPLE** are helped through tissue and eye donation.

Unlike organs, **tissue can be processed and stored for an extended period of time** for use in burn cases, ligament repair, bone replacement and more.

HOW TO BECOME A DONOR

When you get a **DRIVER'S LICENSE** at your local DMV, they will ask if you want to be a donor. If you say YES, you are officially and confidentially added to your state donor registry. Also be sure to share your decision with your family and include donation in your advance directives, will and living will.

You can sign up at **organdonor.gov**.

For more helpful, healthful information, visit **Piedmont.org/LivingBetter**

10 Ways to 'Loosen Up Lighten Up' Infographic

10 Ways to 'Loosen Up Lighten Up'

Be a Blessing Day Graphics

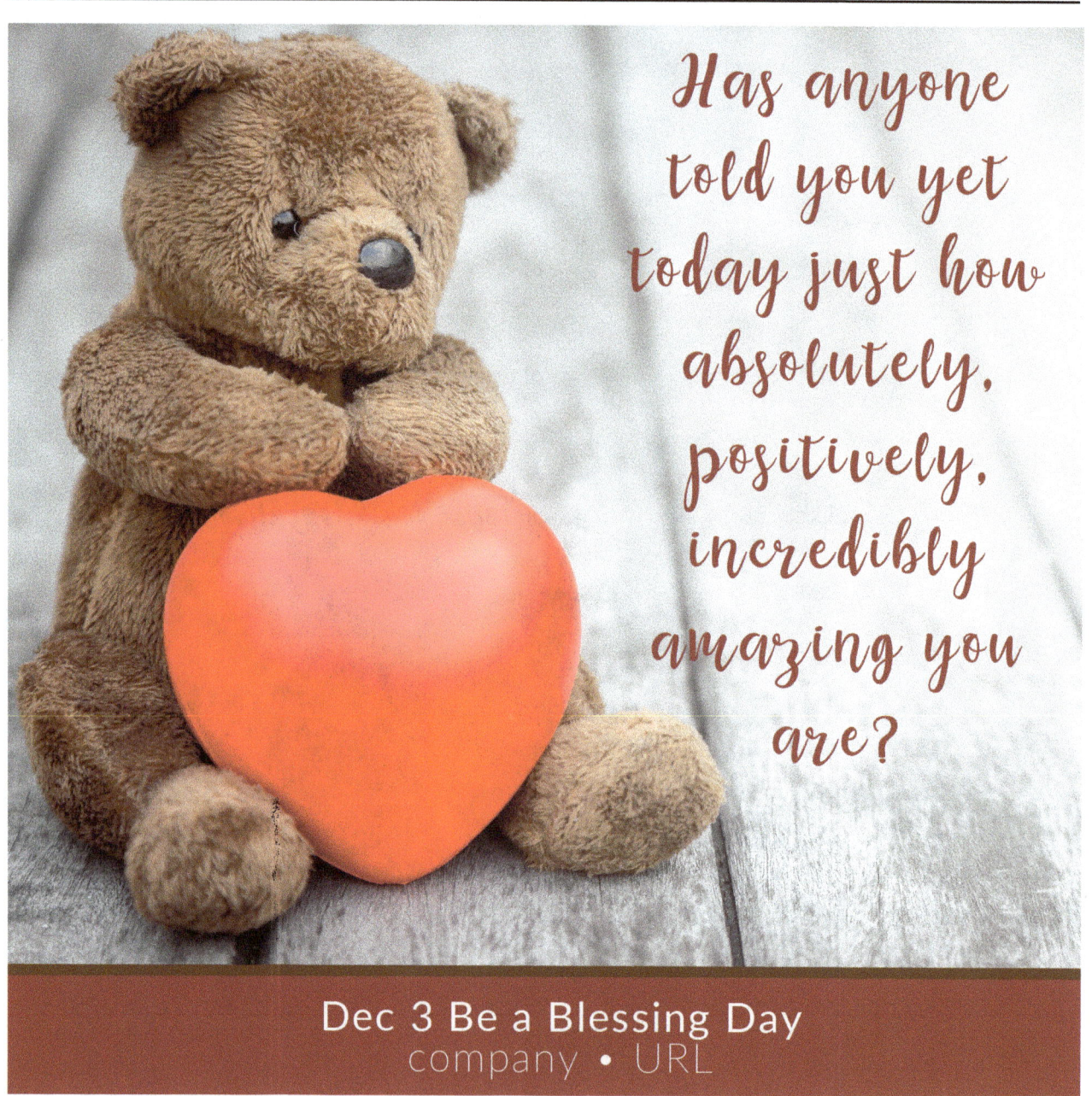

"Irrational Exuberance" Day Graphic

International Mountain Day Graphic

Appendix B: 2020 Social Media Image Size Guide

All dimensions given in pixels.

Facebook

Cover Photo: 820 x 310 (mobile 640 x 320)
Profile Image: 180 x 180 (smartphone 128 x 128)
Fan Page Cover Video 820 x 312
Shared Link: 484 x 252
Shared Square: 1200 will display at 470
Event Image: 1920 x 1080
Ad: 470 x 246 (computer); 560 x 292 (mobile); 254 x 113 (vertical)
Online Display Promotions: 470 x 470 (computer); 626 x 840 (mobile); 254 x 133 (horizontal)

LinkedIn

Profile Image: 400 x 400
Background Image: 1584 x 396
Shared Image: 529 x 320
Shared Image w/link: 520 x 272

YouTube

Channel Profile: 100 x 100
Channel Cover Photo: 2560 x 1440
Video Uploads: 1280 x 720

Instagram

Profile Image: 110 x 110
Photo Thumbnail: 161 x 161
Photo Size: 1080 x 1080
Landscape: 1080 x 566
Portrait: 1080 x 1350
Online Display Promotions: 1080 (square will appear 640);
    1080 x 566 (horizontal will appear 600 x 400)

Twitter

Header Photo: 1500 x 500
Profile Photo: 400 x 400 (displays at 200 x 200)
Timeline Photo: 1024 x 512
Twitter Cards: 800 x 418 pixels or 800 x 800

Pinterest

Profile Image: 280 x 280
Giraffe Pin: 600 x 1560
Pin Sizes: 600 x 750 (portrait); 600 (square); 600 x 900 (optimal); 600 x 1200 (infographic — only one part will appear, clicking will be complete)

Tumbler

Profile Image: 128 x 128
Image Posts: 500 x750

Google+

Profile Image: 250 x 250
Cover Image: 1084 x 610
Shared Image: 530 wide
Shared Link Image: 530 wide

Ello

Banner Image: 1800 x 1300
Profile Image: 340 x 340

SnapChat

Geofilter Image: 1080 x 1920

Chinese Social Media

WeChat
Profile Photo: 200 x 200
Article Preview Header: 900 x 500
Article Preview Thumbnail: 400 x 400 (displays at 200 x 200)
Article Inline Image: 400 wide x any height

Weibo

Cover Image: 920 x 300
Profile Picture: 200 x 200 (displays at 100 x 100)
Banner: 550 x 260
Instream: 120 x 120
Contest Preview: 288 x 288
Contest Picture: 640 x 640
Contest Poster: 570 wide
Prize Picture: 200 x 200

Appendix C: LINKS

Link Checker
For Chrome: https://chrome.google.com/webstore/detail/check-my-links/ojkcdipcgfaekbeaelaapakgnjflfglf?hl=en-GB (I know this is out of alpha order, but a good link deserves top billing, don't you think? ;)

Article Marketing Sites
http://goarticles.com/
http://internationalpractice.com/business/
http://thephantomwriters.com/index.php
http://www.articledashboard.com/
http://www.articlegarden.com/
http://www.articlesbase.com/
http://www.articleson.com/
http://www.sitepronews.com/
http://www.selfgrowth.com
http://marniemarcus.com/unplugged/facebook-ad-management/
http://www.isnare.com
http://www.ladypens.com/
http://www.promotionworld.com
http://www.writeandpublishyourbook.com/magazine/
https://contributor.yahoo.com/signup.shtml
http://www.ezinearticles.com

Auto Responder Services
AWeber: www.aweber.com/
Constant Contact: www.constantcontact.com/
Robly: https://app.robly.com/invite?rc=f56a53fb2ad6910f3e83ebda
Your Mailing List Provider: www.yourmailinglistprovider.com/

Books and Movies
Complete Library of Entrepreneurial Wisdom by Ginger Marks: http://www.CLEWbook.com
A Pirate's Life in the Golden Age of Piracy by Robert Jacob: https://aerbook.com/maker/productcard-3988088-2893.html
Customer Service Skills for Success by Robert W Lucas: http://a.co/d/739PPNL
#Next Level Manners: Business Etiquette for Millennials by Rachel Isgar Ph.D.: http://a.co/cew7qB4
Presentational Skills for the Next Generation by Ginger Marks: http://www.amazon.com/dp/B005EA01QO

Greeting Card Companies
123Greetings: http://www.123greetings.com

American Greetings: http://www.americangreetings.com/
Blue Mountain: www.bluemountain.com/
Cyberkisses: http://www.cyberkisses.com/
Day Springs: www.dayspring.com/ecards/
Evite: www.evite.com
Hallmark: http://www.hallmark.com/
Jacquie Lawson: www.jacquielawson.com/
Just Wink: https://www.justwink.com/
Operation Write Home: http://operationwritehome.org/
Punchbowl Greetings: http://www.punchbowl.com/invitations/preview/5400a4b424e4b36a3e000029/5400a56bbf947f655a000111
Send Out Cards: www.sendoutcards.com/

Podcast Directories

Corante-Podcasting: http://podcasting.corante.com/ — Weblog with news and events related to podcasting.
Hipcast: http://www.hipcaStcom/ — Audio and video podcasting service. Includes news and on-line tour.
iTunes: https://www.apple.com/itunes/ — The iTunes Store puts thousands of free podcasts at your fingertips.
Lextext.com: How to Podcast RIAA Music Under License — http://blog.lextext.com/blog/_archives/2005/1/4/225172.html — Discussion of legal ways to podcast music. [Podcast is 5.3 MB in size]
The Liberated Syndication Network: http://www.libsyn.com/ — Full featured service tailored specifically for media Self-publishing and podcasting. Price is based on usage, changing monthly if needed.
NPR: http://www.npr.org/rss/podcast/podcast_directory.php — Over 50 public radio stations and producers are working with NPR to bring you podcasting.
The Podcast Directory: http://www.podcastdirectory.com/ — Up to date and relevant podcast directory.
Podcasting News: http://www.podcastingnews.com/ — Information relating to podcasting, a podcast directory, and a user forum.
SkypeCasters: http://www.henshall.com/blog/archives/001056.html — Introducing instructions for SkypeCasting, the solution for podcasters to create audio recordings from interviews and conference calls using Skype.
Skype Forums: http://forum.skype.com/viewtopic.php?t=12788 — Recording a Skype Conversation–Discussion thread covering software, techniques, and legal tidbits.
Wikipedia: Podcast –http://en.wikipedia.org/wiki/Podcast — Encyclopedia entry covering basics of the topic.

Promotional Product Supply Companies

4imprint: https://www.4imprint.com/ — offers free samples
Build a Sign: http://www.buildasign.com/
CafePress: www.cafepress.com/
Crown Awards: https://www.crownawards.com/
iPrint: http://www.iprint.com
Judie Glenn Inc: www.judieglenninc.com — ask for Tracey Arehart
Northwest Territorial Mint: http://custom.nwtmint.com/

Overnight Prints: http://www.overnightprints.com/
PC/Nametag˚: http://www.pcnametag.com/
Promotional Products: www.promotionalproducts.org/ — Get free quotes from multiple vendors
Staples: www.StaplesPromotionalProducts.com
VistaPrint: www.Vistaprint.com
World Class Medals: http://www.worldclassmedals.com/
Zazzle: http://www.zazzle.com/custom/buttons

Quote Sources
Bartleby: http://www.bartleby.com/
Brainy Quote: http://www.brainyquote.com/quotes/keywords/resources.html
Leadership Now: http://www.leadershipnow.com/quotes.html
Quote Garden: http://www.quotegarden.com/index.html
Quoteland: http://www.quoteland.com/
The Quotations Page: http://www.quotationspage.com/
Think Exit: http://thinkexist.com/quotes/american_proverb/
Woopidoo!: http://www.woopidoo.com/

Stock Photos
Tiny Eye: http://www.tineye.com — Reverse image search
Alamy: http://www.alamy.com
Beinecke: http://beinecke.library.yale.edu/digitallibrary
Maps Download MrSid: http://memory.loc.gov/ammem/help/download_sid.html
Big Stock Photo: http://www.bigstockphoto.com
Bing: http://www.bing.com
Can Stock Photo: http://www.canstockphoto.com
CreStock: http://www.crestock.com
DepositPhotos: http://depositphotos.com
Digital Scriptorium: http://bancroft.berkeley.edu/digitalscriptorium — public domain
Dreamstime: https://www.dreamstime.com
EJ Photo: http://www.ejphoto.com — Nature photography
Flickr: https://www.flickr.com — Advanced Search (only search on commercial content etc.)
Fotolia: http://www.foltolia.com
Foto Search: http://www.fotosearch.com
Free Digital Photos: http://www.freedigitalphotos.net
Free Photo: http://www.freefoto.com/index.jsp
Getty: http://www.gettyimages.com/
Google: http://www.images.google.com — Use Advanced Search for Usage Rights, labeled with commercial w/modifications
Icon Finder: http://www.iconfinder.com/illustrations
iStockPhoto: http://www.iStockPhoto.com
Jupiter: http://www.jupiterimages.com
Library of Congress: http://www.loc.gov/index.html — American Memory and Prints and Photographs sections
Morguefile: http://morguefile.com
PhotoSpin: https://www.photospin.com/Default.asp?
Pixabay: http://pixabay.com/
Pixadus: http://pixdaus.com

RGB Stock: www.rgbstock.com — more than 95,000 high quality free stock photos, graphics for illustrations, wallpapers, and backgrounds
Scriptorium: http://www.scriptorium.columbia.edu/ public domain
Shutterstock: http://www.shutterstock.com
Stockxchg (FreeImages): http://www.sxc.hu/
ThinkStock Photos: http://www.thinkstockphotos.com/
Top Left Pixel: http://wvs.topleftpixel.com
VectorStock: https://www.vectorstock.com/royalty-free-vectors
Visipix: http://www.visipix.com — lots of Japanese art
Visual Photos: http://www.visualphotos.com
Watercolor Textures: https://lostandtaken.com/downloads/category/paint/watercolor-texture/
WebStockPro: http://www.webstockpro.com/
Wikimedia Commons: http://commons.wikimedia.org/wiki/Main_Page — Check images via languages
Wikipedia Public Domain List: http://en.wikipedia.org/wiki/Wikipedia:Public_domain_image_resources/ public domain
You Work for Them: http://www.youworkforthem.com

Teleconference Companies
What is: www.business.com/directory/telecommunications/business_solutions/conferencing/
Buyer's Guide: www.buyerzone.com/telecom_services/telecon_services/buyers_guide5.html
Free Conference: www.freeconference.com/
Teleconference Live: http://teleconference.liveoffice.com
Teleconferencing Services: www.teleconferencingservices.net/
Wholesale Conference Call: www.wholesaleconferencecall.com/
Yugma Desktop Sharing Software: http://vur.me/gmarks/Yugma/
Zoom: https://www.zoom.us

Virtual Assistant Companies
A Clayton's Secretary (Kathie M Thomas): http://vadirectory.net/
MJ Stern, VA: http://www.mjstern-va.com/ — Specializes in internet marketing
Streamline Your Marketing (Crystal Pina): https://streamlineyourmarketing.com/

Webinar Services
Adobe Acrobat Connect Pro: http://tryit.adobe.com/us/connectpro/universalvoice/?sdid=DNOSU
BrainShark: http://brainshark.com/
Cisco WebEx: http://webex.com/
ClickMeeting: http://www.clickwebinar.com/
Elluminate: http://www.elluminate.com/Products/?id=3
Facebook Live: https://live.fb.com/
Freebinar: http://www.freebinar.com/
Free Conference Calling: https://www.freeconferencecalling.com/
Fuze: http://www.fuzemeeting.com/
GatherPlace: http://www.gatherplace.net/start/
Google+ Hangouts: https://plus.google.com/hangouts
GoToMeeting: https://www.gotomeeting.com/
GoToWebinar: http://www.gotomeeting.com/fec/webinar

IBM Lotus Unyte: https://www.unyte.net/
iLinc: http://www.ilinc.com/
Infinite Conference: http://www.infiniteconference.com/
InstantPresenter: http://www.instantpresenter.com/
Intercall: http://www.intercall.com/smb/
Mega Meeting: http://www.megameeting.com/professional.html
Nefsis: http://www.nefsis.com/
ReadyTalk: http://www.readytalk.com/
Saba Centra: http://saba.com/
SalesForce: https://www.salesforce.com/
StageToWeb: http://www.stagetoweb.com/livE-event–webcasting.html
Tokbox: http://tokbox.com/
Video Seminar Live: http://www.videoseminarlive.com/
Wix: http://www.wix.com/
Yugma: https://www.yugma.com/
Zoho: http://www.zoho.com/meeting/

Appendix D: RESOURCES

Advanced Directives Forms by State — https://www.aarp.org/caregiving/financial-legal/free-printable-advance-directives/

Beavers: Wetlands & Wildlife PowerPoint — https://www.beaversww.org/international-beaver-day/

Brians Common Errors in English Usage — https://public.wsu.edu/~brians/errors/errors.html

Glaucoma Research Foundation — https://www.glaucoma.org/news/glaucoma-awareness-month.php

GoodNet.org (clothes drive) — https://www.goodnet.org/articles/8-tips-on-how-to-organize-successful-clothes-drive

HRSA Organ Donation Form — https://www.organdonor.gov/register.html

List of Dragon Movies — https://en.wikipedia.org/wiki/List_of_dragons_in_film_and_television

Mind Tools (Personal SWOT Analysis) — https://www.mindtools.com/pages/article/newTMC_05_1.htm

National Register of Historic Places — https://www.nps.gov/subjects/nationalregister/features.htm

Pollinator.org Brochures — https://www.pollinator.org/shop/brochures

Pony Express game — https://westernexpansion.mrdonn.org/ponyexpress.html

Remember Me Thrusday — https://remembermethursday.org/

Strunk and White's Elements of Style — http://www.amazon.com/The-Elements-Style-Fourth-Edition/dp/020530902X

Simply Stacie: Free organizational printables: https://www.simplystacie.net/2018/12/get-organized-2019-free-printables/

UPC (respect for chickens day) — https://www.upc-online.org/respect/

Wikipedia Sports Cliches — https://en.wikipedia.org/wiki/List_of_sports_clich%C3%A9s

Watermelon Carving Inspiration — https://www.pinterest.com/WatermelonBoard/watermelon-carvings/

Watermelon Carving Inspiration 2 — https://www.tasteofhome.com/collection/watermelon-carving-ideas/

YourDictionary, poetry — https://examples.yourdictionary.com/types-of-poetry-examples.html

If you found this book interesting, helpful, motivational, fun, or any of the other numerous adjectives that have been used to describe this award-winning book, I would love to read your comments. Please let others know what a valuable asset you have found by leaving your review on your favorite book store website.

If you would like to have a personal coaching session on how you can use this book to market your business send Ginger an email at ginger.marks@documeantdesigns.com and let her know. This valuable coaching service can be purchased for $295.00 per year and includes personal one-on-one coaching two times per year.

Thank you!

About the Author

Having been a business owner for most of her adult life, operating a multi–million-dollar surgical clinic and a local barbecue take-out to list just a couple, have given Ginger Marks the insight needed to assist business owners from all walks of life.

Ginger is the owner of the Calomar, LLC which holds her DocUmeant family of companies. The various entities all work towards a common goal that just happens to be their tagline; "We Make YOU Look GOOD!" Her services include both publishing and digital design assistance. She is proud of the fact that she is able to give high quality, efficient service at a remarkably reasonable rate. It is for this reason she chose to list her publishing company in New York City while residing in Florida.

When Ginger decided to embark on a writing career it was of no surprise to her mother, who herself is a published author. Her love for the arts is what spurred her to hone her talents as a digital designer, offering services to business owners and authors alike.

DocUmeant.net offers editing and writing services; DocUmeantDesigns.com, as you would guess, focuses on designs ranging from websites to book covers and layouts to buttons and business stationary needs; while DocUmeantPublishing.com's focus was begun with the self-published author in mind. Now with ten years of experience in publishing she has built her success in the global community.

Ginger is a member of DesignFirms where she is a top-rated designer, SPANpro (Small Publishers Association of North America), IBPA (International Book Publishers Association), DBW (Digital Book World), and is on the board of FAPA as VP Communications (Florida Authors and Publishers Association).

Most recently, Ginger was awarded for her generous contribution to internet business while helping others achieve their goals in publishing and marketing. The Golden Mouse Award was presented to her by Women In e-Commerce on Oct 28, 2016. In 2012 she was awarded VIP membership to Covington's Who's Who and her publishing company, DocUmeant Publishing, was awarded the 2012 and 2016 New York Award in the Publishing Consultants and Services category by the U.S. Commerce Association (USCA). She recently won the 2015 & 16 Clearwater, FL Design Firm Award and has won book cover design awards and is a multiple award winner for her *Weird & Wacky Holiday Marketing Guide* from FAPA.

In her spare time, she loves to do crafts of all sorts and sing. And yes, she is a little wacky at times too which keeps her fun and inspiring. Ginger lives in Florida where she works side-by-side with her husband, Philip, who is VP Editing for DocUmeant Publishing.

To contact Ginger whether for publish, design, or interviews you may reach her at ginger.marks@documeantdesigns.com or at 727-565-2130.

Additional Works by Ginger Marks

Visit Ginger's Amazon Author Central for more information or to purchase her books.
https://www.amazon.com/Ginger-Marks/e/B005ECOWD0/

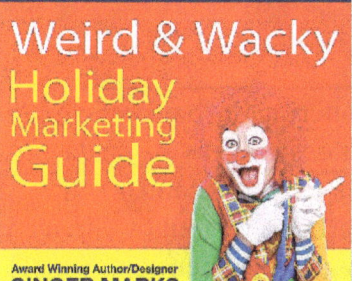

ISBN-13: 978-1937801779

The companion Playbook for the Annual *Weird & Wacky Marketing Guide* l will assist you in planning and tracking your holiday marketing success using the tools, tips, and resources found in the *Weird & Wacky Holiday Marketing Guide*.
- Easily plan and track your marketing
- Organized by month
- Room to write notes
- Track your success
- No expiration date! Start using any time.

Print: $12.97
Available at Amazon.com

Print ISBN:
978-0-9788831-4-0
Digital ISBN:
978-0-9832122-7-0

Much has changed over the years in the public speaking arena. We have so many new and challenging tools at our disposal that we are no longer consigned to countless hours to travel from city to city to share our knowledge.

The internet has opened the doors to people from all places and races. At the click of a button, you can share your information in many forms of multi-media. With the availability of hosting online conferences and collaborations in both text-only and A/V environments, as are offered by Skype Conference™, Hot Conference™ and desktop sharing applications such as Yugma™, as well as teleconferences, the modes and means are so plentiful that more and more savvy business owners are venturing into the public speaking arena.

It is a well thought out, concise, instructional manual written in a manner that all can comprehend. Within the contents of this guide, you will learn the skills necessary to enable you to present your information in such a way that you will capture the attention and hearts of your eager audience.

Available in Print $14.95
Also available in Digital $9.95

$2.99
Kindle Edition
DOWNLOAD:
http://a.co/d/5xP5Ds7

Back to Basics is a collection of articles designed to assist the new business owner to jump start their business or the seasoned profession to put the punch back into their chosen career. It begins with a two-part series on the Nuts and Bolts of Business Building and continues from there to the ever-important Marketing Basics. As marketing is an issue for each and every business owner no matter their business or circumstances this section is presented in three parts. This eBook comes in Kindle and PDF versions and at $2.99 it is a real bargain.

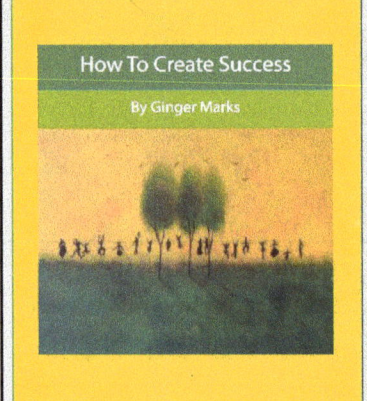

How to Create Success is the first eBook offering. Its bold colorful cover image entitled Jumping for Joy was designed by Amanda Tomasoa of Art by Amanda. The seven chapters contained within combine seven of the most highly rated articles written by Ginger at the time of publishing. One article Contagious Influence is currently the number one requested article and has been published in a magazine for writers titled 'Newbie News'. This is a free ebook and available for immediate download.

FREE to DOWNLOAD: http://www.gingermarksbooks.com/PDFs/HowToCreateSuccess.pdf.

SPECIAL REPORT

How to Create Long Sales Copy Web Pages

DocUmeantDesigns.com

To receive this FREE REPORT sign up for her monthly Words of Wisdom eZine at http://gingermarksbooks.com/.

In this report you will learn how to create an effective Long Sales Copy Web Page and why you might need one. As you read through this report if you come to the conclusion that a Long Sales Copy Web Page is the right tool for your business, I highly recommend you use the company or individual with the working knowledge and integrity to create the site you need to get your important message across to your target market.

If you haven't a clue how to decipher who your target market is then that it the best place to start. Without this knowledge, no matter how compelling your product or service message is, it will result in an ineffective campaign. This will end up costing valuable time and money. Although this is beyond the context of this Special Report there are a myriad of resources available to you today online to help you along the way. As well, there are coaches who specialize in this area of expertise. Feel free to contact me and I will be happy to point you in the right direction.

Additional Works by Ginger Marks | 147

Discover the 10 truths every business owner should know. Knowing and applying these truths will aide you in achieving your dream of entrepreneurship.

©2008 Ginger Marks All rights reserved.

To receive this eBook along with Ginger Marks' report *How to Create Long Sales Copy Web Pages* sign up for her monthly *Words of Wisdom eZine* at http://gingermarksbooks.com/.

DOWNLOAD: http://clewbook.com/

Get your copy of Ginger's *Free Special Report: 10 Easy Steps to Re-purpose Your Content*. This is the insider's view of how the Complete Library of Entrepreneurial Wisdom came about. With the information you will garner in this Special Report, you too can quickly and easily create your very own new money maker.

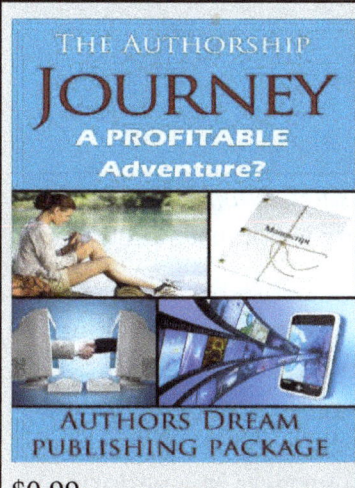

$0.99
Kindle Edition
DOWNLOAD: http://a.co/d/3kRWOkf

The journey to authorship is a road few travel. Find out how you too can traverse the challenges that lie ahead and come out on top. Advice from leading experts in the field.

BUSINESS & PERSONAL GROWTH

Hardcover ISBN: 978-1937801380
Paperback ISBN: 978-1494928292

The Complete Library of Entrepreneurial Wisdom covers business basics, including how to and how not to start your business; marketing; marketing design, which is a topic rarely covered; writing, which covers technical, practical, as well as, marketing aspects to writing; and life reflections, such as planning for emergencies and disasters—both natural and man-made.

With over 150, power-packed, articles to choose from, the busy entrepreneur has at their fingertips, bite-sized training lessons to help them on their success journey. There is so much information packed into this book that it could well be the only book on core business issues that you will ever need.

$9.97 Kindle
$32.95 Hardcover
$24.95 Paperback

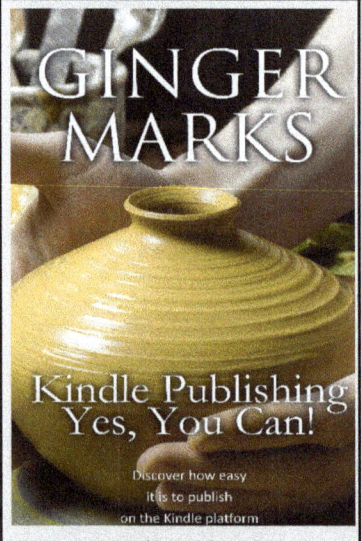

$2.99 Kindle Edition

Publishing your ebook on Kindle doesn't guarantee your book will look the way you intended it to. Even using the Kindle generation tools can result in an ebook that isn't laid out the way you created it. In *Kindle Publishing, Yes You Can*, Ginger Marks, publisher and designer, explains in easy terms exactly what you need to do and how to create an ebook on Kindle that you will be proud to call your own.

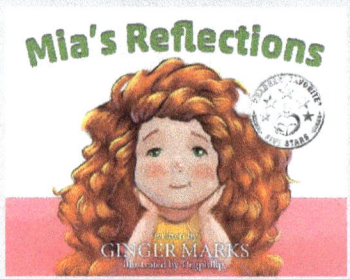

$6.99 Kindle Edition*
$14.99 Print Edition (Feb 2019)

*Available in Fixed & Reflowable formats

Ginger's first children's picture book, *Mia's Reflections* captures the heart of a young girl who learns that beauty is not just a pretty face, but rather a giving life.

Anticipating a new school with no friends, where she feels alone and ugly, young Mia prepares for her first day. She steps near her Grandmother's old Cheval mirror and there she senses her mama reaching out to her. "You're not ugly," her mama says. "You're beautiful." And she traces all the beautiful services Mia performs in a day. At last her mother appears in the mirror to give a fresh look at Mia's loveliness.

Followed by Parent/Teacher resources, this book will fill a young girl's day with thoughts of love and kindness.

Book trailer: https://youtu.be/4DoQe9zp8LY

Additional Works by Ginger Marks | 149

Previous Editions Available at HolidayMarketingGuide.com/past.html
Affiliate Marketing Opportunities available at http://www.HolidayMarketingGuide.com!

www.ingramcontent.com/pod-product-compliance
Lightning Source LLC
Chambersburg PA
CBHW081839170426
43199CB00017B/2783